Learning and Thinking Styles

NEA
SCHOOL RESTRUCTURING SERIES

Learning and Thinking Styles:

Classroom Interaction

Barbara Z. Presseisen

Robert J. Sternberg

Kurt W. Fischer

Catharine C. Knight

Reuven Feuerstein

A Joint Publication
of
National Education Association
and
Research for Better Schools

Robert McClure
NEA Mastery In Learning Consortium
NEA National Center for Innovation
Series Editor

nea **PROFESSIONAL LIBRARY**
National Education Association
Washington, D.C.

Printing History
First Printing: November 1990
Second Printing: February 1993

Note

The opinions expressed in this publication should not be construed as representing the policy or position of the National Education Association or Research for Better Schools. This publication is intended as a discussion document for educators who are concerned with specialized interests of the profession.

Library of Congress Cataloging-in-Publication Data

Learning and thinking styles : classroom interaction / Barbara Z.
    Presseisen . . . [et al.].
        p.   cm.—(NEA school restructuring series)
    "A joint publication of National Education Association [and]
Research for Better Schools."
    Includes bibliographical references (p.).
    ISBN 0–8106–1841–9
    1. Cognitive learning—United States.   2. Cognition in children—
United States.   3. Constructivism (Education)   4. Interaction
analysis in education.   I. Presseisen, Barbara Z.   II. Series.
    LB1590.3.L43   1990
    370.15'2—dc20   90–37219
                                                                   CIP

CONTENTS

As I see it, we are in a battle of paradigms in the history of science, with psychology pitted against the more exact basic sciences that still adhere to the old bottom-up causal determinism and a quantum mechanics view of things.

—Roger Sperry
APA Monitor 21, no. 3:5
March 1990

Chapter 1

IMPORTANT QUESTIONS

by Barbara Z. Presseisen

> *The current school reform movement is the backdrop against which serious problems about schooling in the current world are raised. These problems lead to a variety of questions for educators: What is schooling for? How do students learn? What is intelligence? What makes students intelligent? Can students' abilities be changed? What are the important roles for teachers and educators in an effective school? Answers to these questions are suggested tentatively, but even more importantly, the need to carry these issues further and to examine the work of various researchers on human learning and development is emphasized. Studies from three important cognitive theories are found in the subsequent chapters of this book.*

WHAT PARADIGM FOR EDUCATION?

American education is engaged in a period of major reform, a time of change and reorganization—perhaps an era of reconceptualization and redirection (Cuban 1990). Some writers see these changes as a worldwide recognition that an educational "paradigm shift" is occurring, based on new understandings about how humans develop and learn (de Bono 1989; Gardner 1985). Others see these changes appearing because of new realizations about how societies mature and change (Gardner 1989; Kennedy 1987).

National leaders are calling for change in schooling in

terms of the desire to "restructure" outdated educational bureaucracies, to make schools more effective in a rapidly changing world (Cohen 1988; Kearns and Doyle 1988; Shanker 1990). Their perspective is heavily influenced by the needs of the marketplace and demands of an interdependent and complex industrial society. These leaders tremble at what they believe is a failing American profile of achievement in a competitive, global society. They project that, unless major changes are made now in what schools pursue, dramatic failure lies ahead for the nation, as well as for individual students and workers.

Nearly everyone agrees that change must occur in the classroom itself, in the relationships that exist between the teachers and the taught, in the environment for learning that is experienced by the real performers of achievement, the students themselves (Brandt 1988, Slavin, Madden and Stevens 1989/1990). This need for change is spurred on by an awareness of demographic shifts, of populations of students characteristically different from cohorts of youngsters in the past, reflecting multicultural and ethnic backgrounds of much greater diversity across the nation (Hodgkinson 1985).

Whichever viewpoint one chooses, a period of reform requires that important new questions be raised and, if possible, alternative answers pursued. If we have a new understanding about how learning occurs, what does that mean for the perspectives we had before? If the world is rapidly changing, and similarly the populations we serve in our schools, what does that mean for the assumptions and expectations previously held? If the classroom needs to be redefined, the roles and responsibilities of the teacher altered to relate to that definition, what does that imply for the view of ourselves as educators or of our students as learners? What do all these changes mean to the larger organization of a school system and to its practices in curriculum, instruction, and assessment? These are some of the questions generated by such an educational paradigm shift. They raise many of the compelling issues that underlie the chapters of this book.

The Importance of Human Learning

Questions about current school reform provide the basis for addressing the new, troubling problems that schools must confront in the 1990s. These questions cannot lose sight of the student's perspective of what schooling entails. For education, at its heart, must deal with both teaching *and* learning. Ultimately, human learning and development is the bedrock upon which educators' tasks finally rest. That is what this book is all about. Raising questions that are pressing school leaders today brings into focus basic theories about how children learn and change. What new research is available to help educators understand how students learn? How do students become competent thinkers? What insights about learning ultimately influence a student's progress or determine whether a child's potential is tapped at all? If questions like these are not considered in school reform or restructuring, then, some say, such efforts have not really addressed the most serious problems of the day.

"Restructuring is not the issue," said Ted Sizer of Brown University, who heads the Coalition of Essential Schools. "It's a means to an end—thinking kids. If that leads to restructuring, so be it." (*ASCD Update* 1989, p. 3)

The current reform period is also a time in which much attention has been focused on teaching thinking, on looking not only at basic or essential skills of knowing but at more complex or higher mental operations. For more than a quarter of a century, cognitive science has been expanding into a major interdisciplinary effort that spans artificial intelligence, memory studies, brain research, and creativity in many fields (Diamond 1988; Gardner 1985; Schneider and Pressley 1989; Penrose 1989). Only a part of this "revolution" has touched the goals or programs of American education. It may well be time to consider more fully what a focus on cognitive development means to the education of young people. Developing human resources in schools may relate to looking at teaching as an act that can cultivate the intellectual abilities of *all* students. What do we know about effective schooling that will enable every student to meet the high standards of a technologically sophisticated world? What ought we know about human learning that is key for survival both within and beyond a particular educational institution?

These are some of the issues facing the current period of school reform. They are not a simple menu answerable by a singular response. These heady questions need to be considered in terms of the knowledge about learning that has been pursued around the world for nearly a century. More importantly, these issues ought to be held up to challenging and innovative ideas, to the work of researchers who are capable of responding to such queries—and who are also likely to create a new vision for schooling in the future. Learning in its many dimensions is a significant challenge to the current spate of school reform.

The Care and Feeding of Human Intellect

Past experience tells us that issues concerning children's learning often call into question views that are held about intelligence itself. What is intelligence? Conventional wisdom suggests that intelligence is a special faculty that seems to develop in persons with little influence from experience, relatively untouched by variation across cultures or social classes (Hunt 1979, p. vii). This is a static view of intelligence, resting on an early theory that proposes a model in which there is one general factor, a unified capacity for acquiring knowledge, reasoning, or solving problems (Weinberg 1989). Such a view is the source of the general factor, "g," the powerful, single index called IQ, which has long dominated the psychometric approach to education. Using it, some educators have maintained that children's behavior can be represented by a single score that is set at birth, is relatively unchanging, and is expected to be maintained throughout life. Many educational policymakers have used such an intelligence indicator as a basis for decisions about a student's placement, program, and goals for further education.

In contrast to this conventional view, is a model that interprets mental ability as multiple factors of intelligence—an approach that separates out aspects like verbal skills, problem solving, or social effectiveness. This approach views intelligence as more than a mere product of behavior and more complex than one all-encompassing factor (Gardner 1983). It seeks to elucidate the details and techniques of how people actually think and to locate the various mechanisms by which complex information is processed and used by a particular learner (Brown and Campione 1982). Implied in this second model is the potential for variation among individuals and for differences of development even among persons of parallel circumstances or similar heredity. It raises issues such as, if an individual's level of functioning can be modified, then how and by how much? Or, how likely is it that a child will change intellectually because of new or novel experience or as a result of intervention or treatment in schooling that brings about learning? In sum, this second view demands that, as educators, we ask what are the relationships among learning, knowing, and cognitive change in the context of schooling?

In the current reform period, it seems important for educators to examine which conception of intelligence depicts the desirable classroom—the static or dynamic view. What are the implications that these perspectives have for the belief system a given teacher holds about the students in his/her class? And most important, which theory provides an opportunity to develop a given student's *potential*—even amidst social and economic conditions that are lacking and difficult for the educational enterprise to overcome? Which view provides best for optimal learning?

The old nature/nurture controversy may be a significant issue to reexamine while seeking to understand intellectual

11

functioning in children. Does a child's genetic inheritance fix his or her behavior? What about social or cultural factors? Recent research suggests that although heredity does play a significant role in shaping one's personality, attitudes, and behaviors, environments influence the extent to which the full range of genetic reaction is actually expressed (Detjen 1990; Weinberg 1989). Some long-term brain studies indicate that family, school, and society play important roles in providing various settings in which students can learn (Diamond 1988). It follows that teachers can be very important figures in these settings and can be initiators of activities that facilitate optimal learning outcomes for students. Teachers also can be inhibitors of growth. The issue here is not one of nature versus nurture, but the interaction of nature *and* nurture, and a focus on the quality of learning in any given classroom. Educators need to be concerned, it would seem, with the extent to which every learner makes the most of whatever innate ability he/she has the propensity to develop in a given educational setting.

In the long run, one must ask what kind of learning environment is ultimately provided in the schools? Are these buildings "user friendly," intellectual communities? Can a learner venture a question or comment without the fear of reprimand or ridicule? Can the student use a preferred style of learning or must he/she be constrained by one mandated mode, a singular form of approved expression? The view of intelligence that a teacher holds can be modeled in the environment he/she creates for learners to thrive in (Kamii 1984). It is a central factor in setting the expectations an instructor holds for student learning. Unfortunately, where expectation is low, students will wilt, fade, or escape into anonymous collections of the uncritical, for whom schooling is merely a compromised and boring experience (Sizer 1984).

Last but not least, what is the role of the teacher in creating environments for learning and exploration? If students come to school with many different backgrounds, at many levels of preparation and experience, both alien to and unchallenged by the majority culture, how does a creative instructor organize his/her work? What means of presentation will be most effective? What different assumptions need to be made and what kinds of expectations are realistic and adequate? Learning is no longer a simple stimulus/response system. Teaching is no longer the transfer of discrete bits of knowledge, information accumulated in traditional packages and programs, presented in unchanging, universally recognized, units of print.

It is not easy to live through a paradigm shift. Moments of anxiety and frustration seem to abound. Can we be like the legendary Otto von Bismarck and turn our problems into opportunities for change? If we do, where can we look for help? The work of three theorists of human learning and intelligence offer a place to begin. Their observations of students striving to achieve can be studied to look for answers to some of the questions posed in this changing educational world.

Three Theories, Three Visions

The theorists whose chapters follow in this book see children's development and learning in different ways. Robert Sternberg, Kurt Fischer and Catharine Knight, and Reuven Feuerstein are scientists quite removed from each other, working at different universities around the globe. Yet they have a somewhat similar focus and all raise issues concerning student learning and problems of current schooling. They particularly address questions regarding the difficulties that have long plagued educators' attempts to school all the children in a given society.

Robert Sternberg is intrigued by individual differences, as represented by the myriad of student types in every classroom. He maintains that such differences are not tied merely to ability levels, but that learning is very much involved with students' styles, with "the ways in which they prefer to use their intelligence" (Sternberg 1990, p. 366). Styles, the Yale psychologist suggests, are keys to understanding student performance. Sternberg also raises issue about the role of emotion and socialization in learning particular styles, and he stresses the teacher's role in modeling or mentoring in the classroom (Shaughnessy 1989).

Kurt Fischer and Catharine Knight focus on the student's acquisition of skill through different developmental pathways. They maintain there are close relationships among a child's capacity, motivation, and emotional state, and they carefully examine the particular contexts within which student behavior emerges. Fischer and Knight draw a distinction between students' optimal and more middling or real performance, calling on concepts of familiarity, practice, and contextual support as factors that influence the two types of behavior. These researchers stress the significance of developmental levels, tied to particular skill mastery, in the tension between optimal and real performance. They set the stage for a rich discussion about environments for learning and related teaching roles, as well as opportunities for fostering learning in school settings.

Reuven Feuerstein presents his theory of cognitive modifiability based on nearly half a century of research and practice in many corners of the world. The application of his theory has long been noted in current educational works on intellect and teaching thinking (Link 1985). Feuerstein wastes no time in taking the position that, indeed, human beings can be changed—even up to their last moment of life. It is mediation between teacher and learner that holds the key to such modifiability, he contends. But for the Israeli psychologist, mediation does not mean mere exposure. If we intend for a student to learn, to become modified, there are particular ways and specific conditions that need to be brought into the learner's purview. Feuerstein has developed a major program, *Instrumental Enrichment*, for creating such teachable situations. Like Sternberg, he examines the role of culture and socialization as

14

important aspects of making such a program operational.

What might these various views offer to the questions we raise concerning reform? Each of these three research theories brings new insights and optimism to the vexing and long-standing difficulties that plague attempts to educate all the children of an industrial society. Collectively, these innovative researchers suggest that a broadly based understanding about children's cognitive processing in learning is beginning to emerge. Caught up in this period of reform, it behooves us to read each of their presentations to see if the questions we must pose about schooling and learning can be better understood from these theorists' perspective, experience, and research.

Some might say that a reading task as suggested by this book only addresses highly theoretical questions of the psychology of learning most teachers left behind long ago in graduate school. The sad fact is that many educators have never addressed such questions. Nevertheless, today the responsibilities of their occupation require *professional* educators to consider seriously issues of student learning and development, as presented by the three theories in this study. The most *practical* understandings about students and achievement lie behind issues such as intelligence, modifiability, and teacher mediation. Reading this volume may prove to be a serious examination for teachers, administrators, policymakers, and teacher educators to complete. In their thoughtful consideration, and more importantly, in discussions about the issues in this volume with their peers and colleagues, the major reform of education in America's schools may (or may not) actually occur.

REFERENCES

Association for Supervision and Curriculum Development. 1989. Miniconference report. *ASCD Update* 31, no. 2: 3.

Brandt, R. 1988. On changing secondary schools: A conversation with Ted Sizer. *Educational Leadership* 45, no. 5: 30–36.

Brown, A. L., and Campione, J. C. 1982. Modifying intelligence or modifying cognitive skills: More than a semantic quibble? In *How and how much can intelligence be increased?* ed. D. K. Detterman and R. J. Sternberg. Norwood, N.J.: Ablex.

Cohen, M. 1988. *Restructuring the education system: Agenda for the 1990s.* Washington, D.C.: Center for Policy Research, National Governors Association.

Cuban, L. 1990. Reforming again, again, and again. *Educational Researcher* no. 1: 3–13.

de Bono, E. 1989. *The direct teaching of thinking in education and the CoRT Method.* Paris: Organization for Economic Cooperation and Development, Centre for Educational Research and Innovation.

Detjen, J. 1990, February 16. Stronger link found for genes, behavior. *Philadelphia Inquirer*, pp. 1, 10-A.

Diamond, M. C. 1988. *Enriching heredity: The impact of the environment on the anatomy of the brain.* New York: Free Press.

Gardner, H. 1989. *To open minds.* New York: Basic Books.

Gardner, H. 1985. *The mind's new science: A history of the cognitive revolution.* New York: Basic Books.

Gardner, H. 1983. *Frames of mind: The theory of multiple intelligences.* New York: Basic Books.

Hodgkinson, H. L. 1985. *All one system: Demographics of education, kindergarten through graduate school.* Washington, D.C.: Institute for Educational Leadership.

Hunt, J. M. 1979. Foreword. In *The dynamic assessment of retarded performers: The learning potential assessment device, theory, instrument, and techniques,* ed. R. Feuerstein, Y. Rand, and M. B. Hoffman, vii–xi. Glenview, Ill.: Scott, Foresman.

Kamii, C. 1984. Autonomy: The aim of education envisioned by Piaget. *Phi Delta Kappan* 65, no. 6: 410–15.

Kearns, D. T., and Doyle, D. P. 1988. *Winning the brain race: A bold plan to make our schools competitive.* San Francisco: Institute for Contemporary Studies Press.

Kennedy, P. 1987. *The rise and fall of great powers: Economic change and military conflict from 1500 to 2000.* New York: Random House.

Link, F. R., ed. 1985. *Essays on the intellect.* Alexandria, Va.: Association for Supervision and Curriculum Development.

Penrose, R. 1989. *The emperor's new clothes: Concerning computers, minds, and the laws of physics.* New York: Oxford University Press.

Schneider, W., and Pressley, M. 1989. *Memory development between 2 and 20.* New York: Springer-Verlag.

Shanker, A. 1990. The end of the traditional model of schooling—and a proposal for using incentives to restructure our public schools. *Phi Delta Kappan* 71, no. 5: 345–57.

Shaughnessy, M. F. 1989. An interview with Robert J. Sternberg. *Human Intelligence Newsletter* 10, no. 2: 1–3.

Sizer, T. R. 1984. *Horace's compromise: The dilemma of the American high school.* Boston: Houghton Mifflin.

Slavin, R. E.; Madden, N. A.; and Stevens, R. J. 1989/1990. Cooperative learning models for the 3R's. *Educational Leadership* 47, no. 4: 22–28.

Sternberg, R. J. 1990. Thinking styles: Keys to understanding student performance. *Phi Delta Kappan* 71, no. 5: 366–71.

Weinberg, R. A. 1989. Intelligence and IQ. In *American Psychologist*, ed. F. D. Horowitz. Special issue: Children and their development: Knowledge base, research agenda, and social policy application, 44, no. 2: 98–104.

Chapter 2

INTELLECTUAL STYLES: THEORY AND CLASSROOM IMPLICATIONS*

by Robert J. Sternberg

This chapter presents a theory of intellectual styles and discusses its relevance for education. This theory concerns itself not with intelligence per se but rather with how people use their intelligence. *It is based on a notion of mental self-government, according to which people, like societies, survive by instituting one of several alternative forms of governance. People do not have one style exclusively, rather they show various preferences, which vary somewhat as a function of the particular situation a person is in. Schools overwhelmingly favor certain intellectual styles over others and often confuse style with level of intellect. The styles are described, and their implications for the classroom discussed.*

Throughout my four years in college my two roommates and I remained together. The three roommates—Alex, Bob, and Cyril (only one of these names is unchanged)—seemed remarkably similar intellectually when they entered college. All had high Scholastic Aptitude Test scores, excellent grades in high

*Preparation of this chapter was supported by Contract MDA90385K0305 from the Army Research Institute. Requests for reprints should be sent to Robert J. Sternberg, Department of Psychology, Yale University, Box 11A Yale Station, New Haven, CT 06520.

school, and similar intellectual strengths and weaknesses. For example, all three were more verbal than quantitative; they reasoned well but were rather weak spatially. Thus, in terms of standard theories of intelligence, the three roommates had similar intellectual abilities. Moreover, today, all three roommates are successful in their jobs and have achieved some national recognition for their work, showing that the three roommates had similar motivational levels as well.

However, one who looks beyond the intellectual similarities of the three roommates cannot help but notice some salient differences, which have profoundly affected their lives. Consider some of the differences among Alex, Bob, and Cyril.

Alex, a lawyer, is admittedly fairly conventional, rule-bound, and comfortable with details and structure. He does well what others tell him to do, as a lawyer must, and has commented to me that his idea of perfection would be a technically flawless legal document or contract such that those who sign on the dotted line are bound to the terms of the contract without loopholes. In a nutshell, Alex is a follower of systems—and he follows them extremely well, as shown by the facts that he was a Rhodes Scholar and that he is today a partner in a major national law firm. Alex can figure out a system and work excellently within it.

Bob, a university professor, is quite different stylistically from Alex. He is fairly unconventional and, unlike Alex, dislikes following or even dealing with other people's rules. Moreover, he has relatively few rules of his own. Although he has some basic principles that he views as invariants, he tends not to take rules very seriously, viewing them as conveniences that are meant to be changed or even broken as the situation requires. Bob dislikes details and generally is comfortable working within a structure only if it is his own. He does certain things well—but usually only if they are things he wants to do rather than things someone else wants him to do. His idea of intellectual perfection would be the generation of a great idea and a compelling demonstration

19

that the idea is correct, or at least useful. In brief, Bob is a creator of systems and has designed some fairly well-known psychological theories that reflect his interest in system creation.

Cyril, a psychotherapist, is like Bob, but not Alex, in that he is fairly unconventional. Like Bob, he dislikes others' rules, but, unlike Bob, he has a number of his own. He tends to be indifferent to details. He likes working within certain structures, which need not be his own, but the structures must be ones he has adjudged to be correct and suitable. Cyril does well that which he wants to do. His idea of perfection would be a difficult but correct psychological diagnosis, followed by an optimal psychotherapeutic intervention. In sum, Cyril is a judge of systems. His interest, perhaps passion, for judging was shown early in his career when, as a college student, he constructed a test (which we called the "Cyril Test") to give to others, and especially to dates, to judge the suitability of their values and standards. Cyril was also editor of the college course critique, a role in which he took responsibility for the evaluation of all undergraduate courses at the university.

Although Alex, Bob, and Cyril are all intellectually able and similarly competent, even these brief sketches serve to illustrate that they use their intelligence in different ways. Alex is a follower or executor, Bob, a creator or legislator, and Cyril, a judge of systems. They differ in terms of their intellectual styles—that is, the ways in which they direct their intelligence. A style, then, is not a level of intelligence but a way of using it—a propensity. When one is talking about styles rather than levels, one cannot talk simply about better or worse. Rather, one must speak in terms of better or worse *for what?*

THE MODEL OF INTELLECTUAL STYLE AS MENTAL SELF-GOVERNMENT

I am proposing here a model of intellectual style as mental self-government. The basic idea underlying this model is that governmental structures may be external, societal manifestations of basic psychological processes that are internal and individual (see also Bronfenbrenner 1977). Seeds of this notion can be found in the writings of such political theorists as Hobbes, Locke, and Rousseau whose political theories were based on psychological theories of what people are like. The difference here, perhaps, is that rather than attempting to understand governments in terms of the psychology of human beings, we are trying to understand the psychology of human beings in terms of governments. From this point of view, government in society is a large-scale, externalized mirror of the mind. People are systems, just as societies are (Ford 1986), and they need to govern themselves just as societies do. Mental incompetence results from a breakdown of self-regulating functions, while high levels of mental competence derive in part from superior self-regulation.

The view of intellectual style as mental self-government focuses more on uses than on levels of intelligence. In standard theories of intelligence, including recent ones (Gardner 1983; Sternberg 1985a), the emphasis is on levels of intelligence of one or more kinds. Measuring intelligence thus entails assessing how much of each ability the individual has. In contrast, the governmental model leads to assessment not of how much intelligence the individual has but rather of how that intelligence is directed, or exploited. Two individuals of equal intelligence, measured by any of the existing theories of intelligence, might nevertheless be viewed according to this theory as intellectually quite different because of the ways in which they organize and direct that intelligence. In the next part of this chapter the implications of the mental self-government model as a basis for understanding intellectual styles are explored in some detail.

Governments have many aspects, such as function, form, level, scope, and leaning. Three major functions of government are the legislative, the executive, and the judicial. Four major forms of government are the monarchic, the hierarchic, the oligarchic, and the anarchic. Two basic levels of government are the global and the local. Two domains in the scope of

21

government are the internal (domestic affairs) and the external (foreign affairs). Finally, two leanings are conservative and progressive. In this part of the chapter, the implications of each of these aspects for understanding intellectual styles are explored.

The Functions of Mental Self-Government

Governments can be viewed as having three primary functions: legislative, executive, and judicial.

The legislative style characterizes individuals who enjoy creating, formulating, and planning for problem solution. Such individuals, like Bob the university professor described earlier, want to create their own rules, enjoy doing things their own way, prefer problems that are not prestructured or prefabricated, and like to build structure as well as content in deciding how to approach a problem. People with legislative tendencies prefer creative and constructive planning-based activities, such as writing papers, designing projects, and creating new business or education systems. They tend to enter occupations that enable them to utilize their legislative style, such as creative writer, scientist, artist, sculptor, investment banker, policy maker, and architect.

Individuals with an executive style are implementers. Like Alex the lawyer, they want to follow rules and work within existing systems, preferring prestructured or prefabricated problems that allow them to fill in content within existing structures. They prefer predefined activities, such as solving algebra word problems or engineering problems, giving talks or lessons based on others' ideas, and enforcing rules. Executive types gravitate toward such occupations as lawyer, police officer, builder (of others' designs), surgeon, soldier, proselytizer (of others' systems), and manager (lower echelon).

The judicial style, as shown by the psychotherapist Cyril, involves judgmental activities. Judicial types like to analyze and criticize, preferring problems in which they evaluate the structure and content of existing things and ideas. They prefer activities that exercise the judicial function, such as writing critiques, giving opinions, judging people and their work, and evaluating programs. People with a primarily judicial style tend to gravitate toward such occupations as judge, critic, program evaluator, admissions officer, grant or contract monitor, systems analyst, and consultant.

People do not have one or another style exclusively—rather, they tend to specialize, some people more than others. For example, one individual might be strongly legislative and only weakly executive and judicial, whereas another individual might be approximately equally balanced among the three functions. Thus, people differ not only in the direction of their specialization but also in the degree to which they specialize. People will gravitate toward problems with solutions that require their preferred styles of functioning. They might also use certain styles in the service of other styles. A primarily legislative type, for example, might use judicial functions primarily to further legislative ends.

We need to distinguish people's proclivity toward a style from their abilities to implement that style. It seems likely that most people will prefer styles that capitalize on their strengths. But there is no logical or psychological reason why preferences and abilities will always correspond. Some people might prefer styles that are not as well suited to their abilities as others are. In measuring styles it is important to measure both predilections toward styles and abilities to implement them in order to determine how well an individual's predilections and abilities match.

An important implication of these differences is that although style is generally independent of level of intelligence, it probably is not independent of level of intelligence within a particular domain. The same individual who might be thought to be a brilliant science student because he is a legislative type might be thought to be somewhat duller in business courses that place more emphasis on executive skills.

23

The Forms of Mental Self-Government

Governments come in different forms. Four of these forms are the monarchic, the hierarchic, the oligarchic, and the anarchic. Logically, any form can be paired with any function, although, psychologically, certain pairings are likely to be more common than others.

People who exhibit a predominantly monarchic style tend to be motivated by one goal or need at a time. Single-minded and driven, they often believe that the ends justify the means and attempt to solve problems full-speed ahead—damn the obstacles. Monarchic types are relatively unself-aware, intolerant, and inflexible and have relatively little sense of priorities and alternatives. They tend to oversimplify problems and are often more decisive than the situation warrants. In a limited sense they may be systematic; however, they may neglect variables not obviously pertinent to their goal.

Individuals preferring a hierarchic style tend to be motivated by a hierarchy of goals, recognizing that not all goals can be fulfilled equally well and that some goals are more important than others. They take a balanced approach to problems, believing that ends do not justify means and viewing competing goals as acceptable (although they might have trouble if the priorities come too close to allow for the formation of a hierarchy). Hierarchic types seek complexity and tend to be self-aware, tolerant, and relatively flexible. They have a good sense of priorities, are usually decisive (unless priority setting becomes a substitute for decision or action), and are systematic in problem solving and decision making.

Those who prefer the oligarchic style tend to be motivated by multiple, often competing goals of equal perceived importance. Plagued by multiple, possibly competing, approaches to problems, they are often driven by goal conflict and tension arising out of their belief that satisfying the constraints is as important as solving the problem itself. They usually believe that ends do not justify means and find that competing goals and needs tend to interfere with task completion because each goal and need are seen as having roughly equal importance. Oligarchic types seek complexity (sometimes to the frustration point) and are self-aware, tolerant, and very flexible. They tend to have trouble setting priorities because everything seems equally important, and, thus, they are rather indecisive and multiply systematic, with the multiple systems competing with each other because of the need to satisfy several equally important goals.

Anarchic stylists tend to be motivated by a potpourri of needs and goals that are often difficult for themselves, as well as others, to sort out. They take a random approach to problems, driven by what seems to be a muddle of inexplicable forces. They might act as though ends justify means, for lack of other standards. Anarchic types are often unclear or unreflective on their goals, overly simplistic, unself-aware, intolerant, and too flexible. They might believe that anything goes and have trouble setting priorities because they have no firm set of rules on which to base them. They tend to extremes, being either too decisive or too indecisive, and are thoroughly asystematic.

Some general issues arise with regard to formal style of mental self-government. Monarchists will often be too single-minded for the likes of most teachers and even social acquaintances. But in later life, their single-minded zeal might render them among the most successful of entrepreneurs or goal-attainers. Often their memories of school will not be fond because they will believe that their talents went unrecognized. Monarchists can also be difficult to live with because of their single-mindedness.

Hierarchical types can probably solve the widest variety of problems in school life and beyond because most problems are probably best conceived of hierarchically. They will generally achieve a good balance between thought and action, but they must remember that the existence of priorities does not guarantee that those priorities are right. When there is a serious bottom line, or pressing goal, hierarchists may get lost or sidetracked in their own hierarchies, whereas monarchists may blitz through and attain the goal.

Oligarchists will often frustrate themselves and others, in school and in their careers, because of their indecision and hesitation. Because they tend to assign equal weights to competing means and goals, they may appear to be "lost in thought" and unable to act. They can act, but they may need others to set their priorities for them.

Anarchists are at risk of becoming educational as well as social misfits, and their talents might actually lead them into anti- rather than prosocial paths. Properly nurtured, they might have the potential for making truly creative contributions to the world if their anarchic style is combined with the intellectual talents necessary for creative performance. But proper nurturance can be quite a challenge because of the anarchists' unwillingness to work within existing systems in order eventually to go beyond these systems. Rather than working within existing systems, anarchists might end up attempting to destroy them.

The Levels of Mental Self-Government

Globalists prefer to deal with relatively large and abstract issues. They tend to ignore or dislike detail, choosing instead to conceptualize and work in the world of ideas. Their weaknesses are that they may be diffuse thinkers who can get lost on "Cloud 9" and that they might see the forest but not always the trees within it.

In contrast, localists like concrete problems that require detailed work and are often pragmatically oriented and down-to-earth. Their weakness, however, is that they might not see the forest for the trees.

In terms of the three individuals described earlier, Bob and Cyril tend to be globalists, whereas Alex tends to be a localist. The local style is not, however, inextricably linked to the executive style Alex has shown. Some executive types may prefer to work only at a broader level, accomplishing the main tasks in a project while relegating the more local details to others. Similarly, a legislative or judicial type could be more local than either Bob or Cyril.

Although most people prefer to work at either a more global or a more local level, a key to successful problem solving in many situations is being able to traverse between levels. Thus, it is often helpful to pair a person who is weak within a given level with someone whose strengths are complementary. In particular, although we often value most those people who are most like ourselves, we actually benefit most from those people who are moderately unlike ourselves with respect to preferred level of processing. If there is too much overlap, some levels of functioning might simply be ignored. Two globalists, for example, might do well in forming ideas but will need someone to take care of the details of implementing them. Two localists might help each other in implementation but first need someone to set down the global issues that need to be dealt with. If there is too little overlap, however, a breakdown in communication can occur. People who do not overlap at all in levels might not be able to understand each other well.

The Scope of Mental Self-Government

Governments need to deal both with internal, or domestic, affairs and with external, or foreign, ones. Similarly, mental self-governments need to deal with both internal and external issues.

Internalists tend to be introverted, task-oriented, aloof, socially less sensitive, and interpersonally less aware than externalists. They also like to work alone. Essentially, their preference is to apply their intelligence to things or ideas in isolation from other people.

Externalists tend to be extroverted, people-oriented, outgoing, socially more sensitive, and interpersonally more aware than internalists. They like to work with others and seek problems that either involve working with other people or are about others.

Among the three individuals described earlier, Alex and Bob tend more toward the internal scope of mental self-government, whereas Cyril tends more toward the external. These proclivities fit with their jobs. Alex works primarily in corporate law, dealing more with legal principles and documents and less with people; Bob works primarily with ideas and instantiating them through experiments; Cyril, as a psychotherapist, is constantly working with people. It should be realized that some degree of situation-specificity is involved. Bob, for example, works actively with students and frequently gives lectures on his work. At the same time, he tends to shun parties and generally prefers to deal with people socially when there is at least some degree of task orientation. Moreover, he recognizes the importance of dealing with people on his job and makes sure that whatever his preferred tendencies are, he gets the job done when interactions with people are required.

Some people prefer to be internalists, whereas others prefer to be externalists. Again, most people are not strictly one or the other; rather, they alternate between levels as a function of the task, situation, and people involved. But it is important to realize in education and job placement that a bright individual who is forced to work in a mode that does not suit him or her may perform below his or her capabilities.

The Leanings of Mental Self-Government

Governments can have various leanings. For our present purposes, two major "regions" of leanings will be distinguished; conservative and progressive.

Individuals with a predominantly conservative style like to adhere to existing rules and procedures, minimize change, and avoid ambiguous situations whenever possible. They prefer familiarity in life and work.

Individuals with a progressive style like to go beyond

existing rules and procedures, maximize change, and seek, or at least accept, ambiguous situations. They prefer some degree of unfamiliarity in life and work.

Although individuals might, on the average, tend to be more conservative or progressive in their mental self-government, some degree of domain-specificity is clearly involved. For example, an individual who is conservative politically will not necessarily be conservative in her or his personal life; the same will be true for a progressive. Thus, in evaluating styles, and especially leanings, tendencies within particular domains must be taken into account. Moreover, leanings might well change over time as people feel more or less secure in their environments. An individual who is new to an environment might tend to adapt conservatively, whereas an individual who has been in that environment longer might feel more free progressively to attempt to shape the environment. This aspect of style can be among the most mercurial of the various aspects.

DEVELOPMENT OF INTELLECTUAL STYLES

Where do these various modes of intellectual functioning come from? It is possible that at least some portion of stylistic preference is inherited, but I doubt that it is a large part. Rather, styles seem to be partly socialized constructs, just as intelligence is (Sternberg and Suben 1986). From early on, we perceive that certain modes of interaction are rewarded more than others, and we probably gravitate toward these modes; at the same time, we are constrained by our built-in predispositions as to how much and how well we are able to adopt these rewarded styles.

Consider some of the variables that are likely to affect the development of intellectual styles.

Culture is the first variable. Different cultures tend to reward different styles. For example, the North American emphasis on innovation ("making the better mousetrap") might lead to relatively greater rewards for the legislative and progressive styles, at least among adults. National heroes in the United States—for example, Edison as inventor, Einstein as scientist, Jefferson as political theorist, Jobs as entrepreneur, and Hemingway as author—often tend to be heroes by virtue of their legislative contribution. Societies that tend to value conformity and the following of tradition, such as Japan, might be more likely to reward executive and conservative styles. A society that emphasizes conformity and tradition to too great a degree might stagnate because of the styles induced into its members.

A second variable is gender. Traditionally, a legislative style has been more acceptable in males than in females. Men were supposed to set the rules, and women to follow them. Although this tradition is changing, the behavior of many men and women does not fully reflect the new values.

Third is age. Legislation is generally rewarded in the preschool young, who are encouraged to develop their creative powers in the relatively unstructured and open environment of the preschool and some homes. Once these children start school, however, the period of legislative encouragement draws rapidly to a close. They are now expected to be socialized into the largely conforming values of the school. The teacher decides what students should do, and students do it, for the most part. Students who do not follow directions and the regimentation of the school are viewed as undersocialized, and even as misfits. In adulthood, some jobs again encourage legislation, even though training for such jobs may not. For example, high school physics and history instruction is usually largely executive, with students answering questions or solving problems that the teacher poses. But the physicist and the historian are expected to be more legislative. Ironically, they might have forgotten how. We sometimes say that students lose their creativity in school. What they might really lose is the intellectual style that generates creative performance.

A fourth variable is parenting style. What the parent encourages and rewards is likely to be reflected in the style of the child. Does the parent encourage or discourage legislation, or judgment, on the part of the child? The parent also exhibits a certain style, which the child is likely to emulate. A monarchic parent, for example, is likely to reward a child who shows the same single-mindedness, whereas an anarchic parent would probably disapprove of any showing of a monarchic style and try to suppress it as unacceptable. Parents who mediate for the child in ways that point to the larger rather than the smaller issues underlying actions are more likely to encourage a global style, whereas parents who do not themselves generalize are more likely to encourage a more local style.

The last variable is kind of schooling and, ultimately, kind of occupation. Different schools, and especially different occupations, reward different styles. An entrepreneur will probably be rewarded for styles different from those for which an assembly-line worker is rewarded. As individuals respond to the reward system of their chosen life pursuit, various aspects of style are more likely to be either encouraged or suppressed.

Obviously, these variables are only a sampling rather than a complete listing of those variables that are likely to influence style. Moreover, any discussion such as this inevitably simplifies the complexities of development, if only because of the complex interactions that occur among variables. Moreover, styles interact with abilities. Occasionally one runs into legislative types who are uncreative, creative people who eschew legislation, hierarchists who set up misguided hierarchies, and so on. But, for the most part, the interactions will be more synchronous in well-adjusted people. According to the triarchic theory of human intelligence (Sternberg 1986a), contextually intelligent people are ones who capitalize on their strengths and either remediate or compensate for their weaknesses. A major part of capitalization and compensation seems to lie in finding harmony between one's abilities and one's preferred styles. People who cannot find such harmony are likely to be frustrated by the mismatch between how they want to perform and how they are able to perform.

31

If styles are indeed socialized, even in part, then they are almost certainly modifiable to at least some degree. Such modification might not be easy. We know little about how to modify intelligence, and we know even less about how to modify intellectual styles. Presumably, when we learn the mechanisms that might underlie such attempts at modification, we will pursue a path similar to that which some educators and psychologists are following in teaching intelligence (e.g., Sternberg 1986a).

We need to teach students to make the best of their intellectual styles. Some remediation of weaknesses is probably possible. But to the extent that it is not, mechanisms of compensation can usually be worked out that help narrow the gap between weak and strong areas of performance. For example, students with one preferred style can be paired with others who have different preferred styles. Ultimately, we can hope that a theory of intellectual styles will serve not only as a basis for a test of such styles but also as a basis for training that maximizes people's flexibility in dealing with their environment, society, and themselves.

OTHER THEORIES OF STYLES

The styles of intellect proposed here are, of course, not the only ones ever to have been proposed. Theories of intellectual styles abound, and although it is not possible to review them exhaustively here, I will cite some pertinent examples.

Myers (1980; see also Myers and McCaulley 1985) has proposed a series of psychological types based upon Jung's (1923) theory of types. According to Myers, there are sixteen types, resulting from all possible combinations of two ways of perceiving (sensing versus intuition), two ways of judging (thinking versus feeling), two ways of dealing with self and others (introversion versus extroversion), and two ways of dealing with the outer world (judgment versus perception). Gregorc (1985) has proposed four main types or styles, based on all possible combinations of only two dimensions—concrete versus abstract and sequential versus random. Taking a more educationally oriented slant, Renzulli and Smith (1978) have suggested that individuals have various learning styles, with each style corresponding to a method of teaching: projects, drill and recitation, peer teaching, discussion, teaching games, independent study, programmed instruction, lecture, and simulation. Holland (1973) has taken a more job-related orientation and has proposed six styles that are used as a basis for understanding job interests as revealed by the Strong-Campbell Interest Inventory (Strong, Campbell and Hansen 1985). Holland's typology includes six "types" of personality: realistic, investigative, artistic, social, enterprising, and conventional.

Intellectual styles represent an important link between intelligence and personality because they probably represent a way in which personality is manifested in intelligent thought and action. Attempts to understand academic or job performance solely in terms of intelligence or personality probably have not succeeded as well as we had hoped because they neglect the issue of intellectual style—the effects of intelligence and personality on each other. Thus, styles might represent an important "missing link" among intelligence, personality, and real-world performance.

MEASUREMENT OF STYLES

Can styles be measured? I believe they can be. We are currently validating an inventory designed to measure intellectual styles. The inventory consists of a series of statements, which students rate on a 1-to-9 scale, depending on the extent to which each statement is viewed as describing the rater. For example, legislatively minded students would be expected to give high ratings to such statements as "If I work on a project, I like to plan what to do and how to do it" and "I like tasks that allow me to do things my own way." Executive types would prefer such statements as "I like to follow instructions when solving a problem" and "I like projects that provide a series of steps to follow to get a solution." Judicial students would affirm such statements as "I like to study and analyze the behavior of others" and "I like projects that allow me to evaluate the work of others."

Measuring styles is a first step toward understanding people's preferences for ways of using their intelligence. Ultimately we hope to be able to teach students to use various styles flexibly in order to optimize the extent to which they can apply their intelligence, both in and out of school.

IMPLICATIONS FOR THE CLASSROOM

On the whole schools most reward executive types—children who work within existing rule systems and seek the rewards that the schools value. To some extent the schools create executive types out of people who might have been otherwise. But whether the rewards will continue indefinitely for these executive types depends in part on career path, which is why school grades are poor predictors of job success. One's ability to get high grades in science courses that involve problem solving, for example, probably will not be highly predictive of later success as a scientist, an occupation in which many of the rewards result from coming up with the ideas for the problems in the first place. Judicial types might be rewarded somewhat more in secondary and especially tertiary schooling, where at least some judgmental activity is required, as in paper writing. Legislative types might not be rewarded, if at all, until graduate school, where one needs to come up with original ideas in dissertation and other research. But some professors—those who want students who are clones or disciples—might not reward legislative types even in graduate school, preferring executive types who will carry out their research for them in an effective, diligent, and nonthreatening way.

The fit between student and teacher, as between principal and teacher, can be critical to the success of the teacher-student system, or of the principal-teacher system. A legislative student and an executive teacher, for example, might not get on well at all. A legislative student might not even get along with a legislative teacher if that teacher happens to be one who is intolerant of other people's legislations. During the course of my career, I have found that although I can work with a variety of students, I probably work best with students whom I now, in retrospect, would classify as legislative. I can also work reasonably well with executive types. I am probably weakest with judicial students, who seem to me to be more eager to criticize than to do research. The general point is that educators need to take into account their own styles in order to understand how these styles influence their perceptions of and interactions with others. Clearly, certain students benefit from certain activities. A gifted executive-type student might benefit more from acceleration, during which the same material is presented at a more rapid pace. A gifted legislative-type student might benefit more from enrichment because the opportunity to do creative projects would be consistent with that student's preferred style of working.

Schools must take into account not only the fit between teacher and student (or principal and teacher) styles but also the fit between the way a subject is taught and the way a student thinks. A given course often can be taught in a way that is advantageous (or disadvantageous) to a particular style. For example, an introductory or low-level psychology course might stress learning and using existing facts, principles, and procedures (an executive style of teaching), or it might stress designing a research project (a legislative style of teaching), or it might stress writing papers, evaluating theories and experiments, and the like (a judicial style of teaching). Little wonder I received a grade of C in my introductory psychology course, taught in the executive style! And, in retrospect, little wonder that in my own psychology courses, I have almost always made the final grade heavily dependent on the design of a research project. My style of teaching was reflecting my own style of thinking, as it does for others. The general principle that style of teaching reflects the teacher's preference is not limited to psychology or even science. Writing, for example, might be taught in a way that emphasizes critical (judicial) papers, creative (legislative) papers, or expository (executive) papers.

Sometimes there is a natural shift in the nature of subject matter over successive levels of advancement, just as there is in the nature of jobs. In mathematics and basic science, for example, lower levels are clearly more executive, requiring the solution of prestructured problems. Higher levels are clearly more legislative, requiring the formulation of new ideas for proofs, theories, and experiments. Unfortunately, some of the students screened out in the earlier phases of education might have succeeded quite well in the later ones, whereas some students who readily pass the initial stages might be ill suited to later demands.

Perhaps the most important point to be made is that we tend to confuse level with style of intelligence. For example, most current intelligence and achievement tests reward the executive style by far the most—they require the solution of prestructured problems. One cannot create one's own problems or judge the quality of the problems on the test (at least not at the time of test). Judicial types get some credit for analytical items, but legislative types benefit hardly at all from existing tests and might actually be harmed by them. Clearly, style will affect perceived competence, but, as noted earlier, style is independent of intelligence in general, although not within particular domains. Style ought to count as much as ability and motivation in recommending job placements, although probably not in making tracking decisions that deal with issues of ability rather than style.

How can a teacher apply the idea of intellectual styles? Consider some examples.

As a first example, suppose you are teaching a literature lesson on Emily Bronte's *Wuthering Heights*. You might choose to lecture on the book, discussing why in the context of Victorian England, a marriage between Catherine Earnshaw and Heathcliff would have been all but impossible. This lecture format will benefit students with an executive style. Or, if your students have also read Henry James's *Daisy Miller*, you might solicit student participation by asking them to compare and contrast the behavior of Catherine Earnshaw toward her lover with that of Daisy Miller toward her lover. The compare-and-contrast format will benefit the judicial student. Or you might ask students to put themselves in Bronte's place, and to formulate an alternative ending to the book in which Earnshaw and Heathcliff are able to overcome stunning obstacles and to come to terms with each other in life rather than in death. This exercise is geared toward students with a legislative style.

As a second example, suppose you are teaching a course on world history and are covering World War II. You want to assess your students' knowledge about and understanding of the war using a one-period test. One way you might test the students is through an executive-style short-answer or multiple-choice test that assesses their recall of facts and also their understanding of some of the major events of the war. For example, you might ask what general commanded the Allied forces in the Battle of the Bulge, or you might ask why the American military was unprepared for the bombing of Pearl Harbor. Alternatively, you might have a judicial-type essay question asking students to evaluate the motives of the Japanese in attacking Pearl Harbor, or to evaluate how the German loss of World War I served as a springboard for the developments that led to the instigation of World War II. Or as a third, legislative, alternative, you might ask students to place themselves in the position of Harry Truman and to construct a scenario for ending World War II that does not involve the bombing of Hiroshima and Nagasaki. Or you might ask them to imagine that they are in the role of a member of the Underground pretending to support and work for the Vichy government in France. They must use their knowledge of the government to describe ways in which they could undermine the collusion of the Vichy government with the Germans without getting caught.

As a third example, suppose you are teaching biological science and are giving an assignment that you wish students to use as a basis for learning about the difference between the respective roles of the left and the right hemisphere of the brain in cognitive functioning. You might ask students to do an executive-style report on any of a number of books that describe differences between the functioning of the two hemispheres. Or you might ask them to evaluate an experiment, in judicial fashion, that purports to show qualitative differences between left and right hemispheres, or to design a test that would separate those who prefer functioning in one hemisphere from those who prefer functioning in the other hemisphere.

Note that unrecognized differences in teachers' and students' intellectual styles, and in the match between them, may result in substantial differences in the way students are perceived by teachers, and also in the way teachers are perceived by students. In our educational process, therefore, we need to be cognizant not only of students' intellectual abilities, but of how these abilities are exploited through intellectual styles.

REFERENCES

Baltes, P. B. 1986. Notes on the concept of intelligence. In *What is intelligence? Contemporary viewpoints on its nature and definition*, ed. R. J. Sternberg and D. K. Detterman, 23–27. Norwood, N.J.: Ablex Publishing Co.

Berry J. W. 1974. Radical cultural relativism and the concept of intelligence. In *Culture and cognition: Readings in cross-cultural psychology*, ed. J. W. Berry and P. R. Dasen, 225–29. London: Methuen.

Berry, J. W. 1980. Cultural universality of any theory of human intelligence remains an open question. *Behavioral and Brain Sciences* 3: 584–85.

Binet, A., and Simon, T. Methodes nouvelles pour le diagnostic du niveau intellectuel des anormaux. *L'Annee Psychologique* 11: 191–244.

Blum, M. L., and Naylor, J. C., eds. 1968. *Industrial psychology; Its theoretical and social foundations.* New York: Harper & Row.

Bronfenbrenner, U. 1977. Toward an experimental ecology of human development. *American Psychologist* 7: 513–31.

Cantor, N., and Mischel, W. 1979. Prototypes in person perception. In *Advances in experimental social psychology*, ed. L. Berkowitz. New York: Academic Press.

Ford M. E. 1986. A living systems conceptualization of social intelligence: Outcomes, processes, and developmental change. In *Advances in the psychology of human intelligence.* Vol. 3, ed. R. J. Sternberg, 119–71. Hillsdale, N.J.: Lawrence Erlbaum Associates.

Gardner, H. 1983. *Frames of mind: The theory of multiple intelligences.* New York: Basic Books.

Gentner, D., and Grudin, J. 1985. The evolution of mental metaphors in psychology: A 90-year retrospective. *American Psychologist* 40: 181–92.

Gregorc, T. 1985. *Inside styles: Beyond the basics.* Maynard, Mass.: Gabriel Systems.

Guilford, J. P. 1967. *The nature of human intelligence.* New York: McGraw-Hill.

Holland, J. L. 1973. *Making vocational choices: A theory of careers.* Englewood Cliffs, N.J.: Prentice-Hall.

Hunt, E. B. 1980. Intelligence as an information-processing concept. *British Journal of Psychology* 71: 449–74.

Jensen, A. R. 1982. Reaction time and psychometric *g*. In *A model for intelligence*, ed. H. J. Eysenck, 93–132. Berlin: Springer-Verlag.

Journal of Educational Psychology. 1921. Intelligence and its measurement: A symposium. *Journal of Educational Psychology* 12: 123–47, 195–216, 271–75.

Jung, C. 1923. *Psychological types*. New York: Harcourt, Brace.

Kagan, J. 1976. *Commentary on "Reflective and impulsive children: Strategies of information processing underlying differences in problem solving."* Monographs of the Society for Research in Child Development, vol. 41, no. 5, serial no. 168.

Keating, D. 1984. The emperor's new clothes: The "new look" in intelligence research. In *Advances in the psychology of human intelligence*. Vol. 2, ed. R. J. Sternberg, 1–45. Hillsdale, N.J.: Lawrence Erlbaum Associates.

Kogan, N. 1983. Stylistic variation in childhood and adolescence: Creativity, metaphor, and cognitive styles. In *Handbook of child psychology*. 4th ed., ed. P. H. Mussen. Vol. 3, *Cognitive development*, ed. J. H. Flavell and E. M. Markman, 630–706. New York: John Wiley.

Laboratory of Comparative Human Cognition. 1982. Culture and intelligence. In *Handbook of human intelligence*, ed. R. J. Sternberg, 642–719. New York: Cambridge University Press.

Maier, N. R. F., ed. 1970. *Problem solving and creativity in individuals and groups*. Belmont, Calif.: Brooks/Cole.

Myers, I. B. 1980. *Gifts differing*. Palo Alto, Calif.: Consulting Psychologists Press.

Myers, I. B., and McCaulley, M. H. 1985. *Manual: A guide to the development and use of the Myers-Briggs type indicator*. Palo Alto, Calif.: Consulting Psychologists Press.

Newell, A., and Simon, H. A. 1972. *Human problem solving*. Englewood Cliffs, N.J.: Prentice-Hall.

Pellegrino, J. W., and Glaser, R. 1980. Components of inductive reasoning. In *Aptitude, learning, and instruction*. Vol. 1, *Cognitive process analyses of aptitude*, ed. R. E. Snow, P. A. Federico, and W. E. Montague, 177–217. Hillsdale, N.J.: Lawrence Erlbaum Associates.

Renzulli, J. S., and Smith, L. H. 1978. *Learning styles inventory.* Mansfield Center, Conn.: Creative Learning Press.

Roediger, H. 1980. Memory metaphors in cognitive psychology. *Memory and Cognition* 8: 231–46.

Simon, H. A. 1976. Identifying basic abilities underlying intelligent performance of complex tasks. In *The nature of intelligence,* ed. L. B. Resnick, 65–98. Hillsdale, N.J.: Lawrence Erlbaum Associates.

Snow, R. E. 1980. Aptitude processes. In *Aptitude, learning, and instruction.* Vol. 1, *Cognitive process analyses of aptitude,* ed. R. E. Snow, P. A. Federico, and W. E. Montague, 27–63. Hillsdale, N.J.: Lawrence Erlbaum Associates.

Spearman, C. 1927. *The abilities of man.* New York: Macmillan.

Sternberg, R. J. 1980. Sketch of componential subtheory of human intelligence. *Behavioral and Brain Sciences* 3: 573–84.

Sternberg, R. J. 1981. Intelligence and nonentrenchment. *Journal of Educational Psychology* 73: 1–16.

Sternberg, R. J. 1982. Natural, unnatural, and supernatural concepts. *Cognitive Psychologist* 14: 451–58.

Sternberg, R. J. 1984. Toward a triarchic theory of human intelligence. *Behavioral and Brain Sciences* 7: 269–87.

Sternberg, R. J. 1985a. *Beyond IQ: A triarchic theory of human intelligence.* New York: Cambridge University Press.

Sternberg, R. J. 1985b. Human intelligence: The model is the message. *Science* 230: 1111–18.

Sternberg, R. J. 1986a. *Intelligence applied: Understanding and increasing your intellectual skills.* San Diego: Harcourt, Brace, Jovanovich.

Sternberg, R. J. 1986b. Intelligence is mental self-government. In *What is intelligence? Contemporary viewpoints on its nature and definition,* ed. R. J. Sternberg and D. K. Detterman, 141–48. Norwood, N.J.: Ablex Publishing Co.

Sternberg, R. J., and Detterman, D. K., eds. 1986. *What is intelligence? Contemporary viewpoints on its nature and definition.* Norwood, N.J.: Ablex Publishing Co.

Sternberg, R. J., and Suben, J. 1986. The socialization of intelligence. In *Minnesota symposia on child psychology.* Vol. 19, *Perspectives on intellectual development*, ed. M. Perlmutter, 201–35. Hillsdale, N.J.: Lawrence Erlbaum Associates.

Sternberg, R. J., and Wagner, R. K., eds. 1986. *Practical intelligence: Nature and origins of competence in the everyday world.* New York: Cambridge University Press.

Strong, E. K., Jr.; Campbell, D. P.; and Hansen, J. C. 1985. *Strong-Campbell Interest Inventory.* Palo Alto, Calif.: Consulting Psychologists Press.

Thurstone, L. L. 1938. *Primary mental abilities.* Chicago: University of Chicago Press.

Valsiner, J. 1984. Conceptualizing intelligence: From an internal static attribution to the study of the process structure of organism-environment relationships. In *Changing conceptions of intelligence and intellectual functioning: Current theory and research,* ed. P. S. Fry, 63–89. New York: North-Holland.

Wagner, R. K., and Sternberg, R. J. 1985. Practical intelligence in real-world pursuits: The role of tacit knowledge. *Journal of Personality and Social Psychology* 49: 436–58.

Wallach, M. A., and Kogan, N. 1965. *Modes of thinking in young children.* New York: Holt, Rinehart & Winston.

Wechsler, D. 1950. *The measurement of appraisal of adult intelligence,* 4th ed. Baltimore: Williams & Wilkins.

Witkin, H. A. 1978. *Cognitive styles in personal and cultural adaptation: The 1977 Heinz Werner lectures.* Worcester, Mass.: Clark University Press.

Zigler, E.; Balla, D.; and Hodapp, R. 1984. On the definition and classification of mental retardation. *American Journal of Mental Deficiency* 89, no. 3: 215–30.

Chapter 3

COGNITIVE DEVELOPMENT IN REAL CHILDREN: LEVELS AND VARIATIONS*

by Kurt W. Fischer and Catharine C. Knight

Cognitive developmental theories have often failed to be helpful in educational practice because they have neglected the naturally rich variations in children's behavior. Skill theory is designed to analyze the development of real children—who vary in capacity, motivation, and emotional state and who act in specific contexts. This theory shows how real children can exhibit both stagelike developmental levels and wide variations in performance. Development moves through a series of cognitive levels, which are evident only under optimal performance conditions. However, children rarely function at their optimum under the conditions for assessment in the schools, as shown by research on arithmetic concepts and higher-order thinking skills. Real children also take different developmental pathways while acquiring skills. In mastering early reading skills, for example, children show several distinct pathways; the pathway for children at risk for reading problems shows important limitations in sound-analysis skills.

*Preparation of this chapter was supported by grants from the Spencer Foundation and the MacArthur Foundation. We would like to thank Susan Harter, Karen Kitchener, and Louise Silvern for their contributions to the arguments here.

Analyses of cognitive development have suffered from scholars' tendencies to think too simply about children's behavior. Theory and research have focused on an extremely limited set of characteristics of children's behaviors, and so they have not captured the naturally occurring rich variations that children show. As a result, their concepts have often failed to be helpful in analyzing the behavior of real children—children who are affected by context and experience and who vary from moment to moment in terms of capacity, motivation, and emotional state (Fischer and Bullock 1984).

One group of scholars, epitomized by Piaget (1983) and Kohlberg (1969), has focused on the search for uniform stages by which to characterize the child. As a result, they have neglected the variations in behavior that occur with changes in the environmental context and the child's state. The roles of task, experience, emotion, and other causes of variation have been omitted from this cognitive developmental framework.

The result has been an inaccurate portrait of the child, showing consistent performance at a stage and uniform movement from one stage to another. Even when the facts of variation have been recognized (and labeled as *decalage*), they have not been explained (Colby et al. 1983; Piaget 1971, p. 11). In educational practice the Piagetians have been able to provide global descriptions of how children's understandings change with age, but they have not been able to help teachers deal with the wide range of natural variations in behavior within and among students.

Another group, epitomized by most information processing approaches to development (e.g., Klahr and Wallace 1976; Siegler 1983), has focused primarily on analyses of tasks, using those analyses to explain changes in behavior. As a result, the consistencies in behavior with development of the child have been neglected. The contribution of the child's general level of understanding has often not even been assessed (e.g., Chi 1978). In educational practice these information processors have been able to provide analyses of behavior on a few specific tasks, but they have not been able to help teachers understand and make use of students' consistencies in behaviors across contexts.

Skill theory is designed to provide a fuller portrait of development, considering the range of behavior across contexts and states. Its central constructs are based on a collaborational or interactive view that child and environment always work together to produce behavior. Children develop skills that they apply in specific contexts and that they can transfer from one context to another. Skill theory provides a set of constructs for characterizing the structures of these skills, the transformations that produce change from one skill to another, and the functional mechanisms that induce variations in behavior across contexts and states (Fischer 1980; Fischer and Pipp 1984; Fischer and Lamborn 1989).

Characteristics that have been considered contradictory in the past are integrated in skill theory: children develop through stages, but their development is at the same time continuous. The behavior of individual children varies widely across contexts, but it is also consistent. Different children move along different developmental pathways, but at the same time they also all move through the same general developmental sequence. In real children these "contradictions" do not exist. A theory that begins to characterize the rich variations in children's behavior quickly eliminates such overly simple dichotomies.

OPTIMAL LEVELS AND THE CONDITIONS FOR DETECTING THEM

One of the central hypotheses of skill theory is that variations of behavior are constrained by an upper limit on the complexity of skills, called the *optimal level*. Children's behavior varies widely across contexts and states, but the variations do not exceed a certain level of complexity. It is this optimal level that consistently changes in a stagelike way, whereas most behavior does not show stagelike change. That is how real children can show both stagelike developmental levels and wide variations in performance.

Development moves through a series of hierarchical optimal cognitive levels, each of which emerges abruptly during a specific age period. Table 1 outlines the seven levels that emerge between two and thirty years of age. (Six additional levels emerge in the first two years of life.) During the childhood years, skills involve representations of concrete objects, events, or people. Children gradually construct more and more complex relations between these representations as they move through the first four levels shown in the table. With the attainment of the fourth level, at about ten to twelve years of age, abstractions concerning intangible concepts emerge from the complex relations of these representations. Then students gradually construct more and more complex relations among these abstractions and, thus, move through the fifth to seventh levels shown in the table.

The optimal levels are not simply characteristics of the child, however. They are simultaneously characteristics of a specific set of environmental conditions. Only under optimal performance conditions—with familiar, well-practiced tasks and contextual support for high-level performance, as well as motivated, healthy children—are the levels evident. Under those conditions children demonstrate stagelike development of capacities in a wide range of skills, such as understanding arithmetic concepts and describing their own personalities.

To illustrate this effect, we will focus on abstract mappings—the fifth level in Table 1. At this level, which typically emerges at fourteen to sixteen years of age in middle-class Americans, adolescents can relate one abstraction to another in a simple relation. The integration of the abstractions is crucial for the demonstration of the mapping.

With arithmetic (limited to positive whole numbers), for example, they can relate the abstract concept of addition to the abstract concept of substraction. Here is an example:

Table 1
Levels of Development in Childhood and Adolescence

Level	Age of Emergence	Examples of Skills
Rp 1: Single representations	18–24 months	Coordination of action systems to produce concrete representations of actions, objects, or agents: • Pretending that a doll is walking • Saying, "Mommy eat toast."
Rp 2: Representational map- pings	3.5–4.5 years	Relations of concrete repre- sentations: • Pretending that two dolls are Mommy and Daddy interacting • Understanding that self knows a secret and Daddy does not know it.
Rp 3: Representational sys- tems (also called Con- crete operations)	6–7 years	Complex relations of sub- sets of concrete representa- tions: • Pretending that two dolls are Mommy and Daddy as well as a doctor and a teacher simultaneously. • Understanding that when water is poured from one glass to another, the amount of water stays the same.
Rp 4/A 1: Single abstractions (also called Formal op- erations)	10–12 years	Coordination of concrete representational systems to produce general, intangible concepts: • Understanding the con- cept of operation of addi- tion • Evaluating how one's par- ents' behavior demon- strates conformity • Understanding concept of honesty as general quality of interaction.

Table 1 (Continued)

Level	Age of Emergence	Examples of Skills
A 2: Abstract mappings	14–16 years	Relations of intangible concepts: • Understanding that operations of addition and subtraction are opposites • Integrating two social concepts, such as honesty and kindness, in the idea of a social lie
A 3: Abstract systems	18–20 years	Complex relations of subsets of intangible concepts: • Understanding that operations of addition and division are related through how numbers are grouped and how they are combined • Integrating several types of honesty and kindness in the idea of constructive criticism
A 4: Principles*	25 Years?	General principles for integrating systems of intangible concepts: • Moral principle of justice • Knowledge principle of reflective judgment • Scientific principle of evolution by natural selection

*This level is hypothesized, but to date there are too few data to test its existence unequivocally.

Note: Table 1 is based on Fischer (1980), Kitchener (1982), and Lamborn (1986). Ages given are modal ages at which a level first appears, based on research with middle-class American or European children. They may differ across cultures and other social groups.

Addition and subtraction are opposites, even though they both involve combining single numbers. With addition, two numbers are put together to make a larger number, like 5 + 7 = 12. But with subtraction, a smaller number is taken away from a bigger one, like 12 –5 = 7. So they combine numbers in opposite ways.

In this explanation, the abstract operations of addition and subtraction are related through opposition.

To test the optimal-level hypothesis for abstract mappings, we examined performance on four different types of arithmetic relations—addition and subtraction, addition and multiplication, division and multiplication, and subtraction and division (Fischer, Pipp and Bullock 1984; Fischer and Kenny 1986). Further tasks were also given to assess the two earlier levels of representational systems and single abstractions.

In our research, eight people from each grade from third grade through the sophomore year of college performed two items to test each type of arithmetic mapping. For these eight problems we predicted that there would be a sudden spurt in performance with the emergence of a new optimal level at fourteen to sixteen years of age. But this spurt would be evident only under optimal conditions. Ordinary performance would not evidence a spurt.

To test these predictions, Fischer and Kenny (1986) tested each student individually under four assessment conditions. First, they answered a specific question about an arithmetic relation, such as "How does addition relate to subtraction?" Second, they were provided with environmental support for high-level performance: they were shown a prototypic answer, an explanation of the relation in a few paragraphs. Then the card was taken away, and they were asked to answer the question again, taking into account what they had just read.

After this second condition, they were told that they would be tested again on the same items in two weeks, and they were encouraged to think about the arithmetic relations in the interim. Two weeks later the same procedure was administered again. The student's initial reply to the question constituted the third assessment. The explanation after they had again read the prototypic answer was the fourth assessment.

The condition most like ordinary performance under the most common kinds of assessments was the first one (Session 1, No support), during which the student gave a spontaneous answer to the question. There was no practice, no opportunity to think about the question for awhile, and no demonstration of a good answer. Here, as shown in Figure 1, performance improved slowly and gradually after ninth grade (fifteen years of age). There was no evidence of a stagelike change. Improvement was continuous and never reached even 40 percent correct.

At the other extreme, the fourth condition (Session 2, Support) showed a dramatic stagelike change. Through ninth grade, no student performed more than one of the eight problems correctly. In tenth grade (sixteen years of age), every student answered all or almost all of them correctly. In the condition that provided optimal conditions—practice and environmental support for a high-level response—there was a true developmental discontinuity, as shown in Figure 1.

The two intermediate conditions showed a gradual transformation from continuous change to discontinuous change. When students were simply shown a prototypic answer in the first session (Session 1, Support), their performance improved dramatically, but it took several years to reach its maximum, and even then it only reached approximately 60 percent correct. When students returned two weeks later and initially answered the questions (Session 2, No support), their performance showed nearly the same discontinuity as the optimal condition.

As these results illustrate, cognitive development is both continuous and discontinuous. Discontinuities take place at certain ages as a new optimal level emerges, but they occur under optimal assessment conditions, not under ordinary, spontaneous conditions.

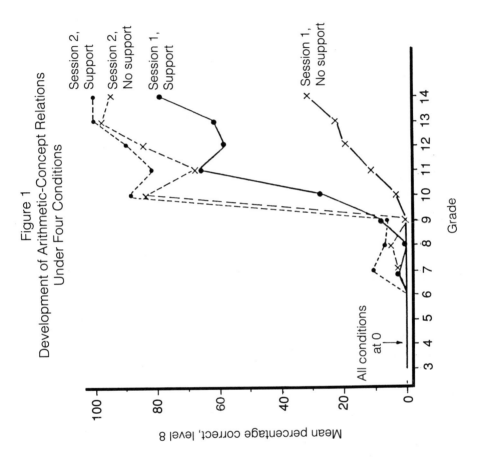

Figure 1
Development of Arithmetic-Concept Relations
Under Four Conditions

According to skill theory, these levels reflect a broad change in capacity, not simply a change in one domain. This capacity change produces, for example, a discontinuity not only in arithmetic relations but also in perceived conflict in one's own personality. With the development of abstractions, adolescents can characterize themselves (as well as other people) in terms of abstract personality characteristics, such as outgoing, outspoken, caring, inconsiderate, and depressed. With abstract mappings these abstract characteristics can be related for the first time, and adolescents can detect conflicts or contradictions in their own personalities.

Based on this argument, we predicted that adolescents would experience a spurt in perceived conflict in their own personalities at fourteen to sixteen years of age. Monsour (1985) and Harter (1986) tested this hypothesis with a structured technique designed to support optimal performance. During individual interviews the adolescents were asked what they were like in a variety of specific situations. Each characterization was written on a small piece of paper with glue on the back, and each adolescent then placed the papers on a drawing of three concentric circles to represent her or his personality. The most important characteristics were put on the inner circle and the least important on the outer circle. The interviewer then asked a series of structured questions intended to determine, among other things, what conflicts the adolescent saw among the characteristics.

Students in the predicted age period showed a dramatic spurt in perceived conflict. Between seventh and ninth grades (thirteen and fifteen years of age), the percentage of students reporting some conflict jumped from 34 to 70 percent, and it remained high in eleventh grade.

Other studies, too, indicate that a new cognitive capacity emerges at this time in development (Fischer and Lamborn 1989). The exact age of emergence will vary across assessment conditions, and it might vary across social groups. But at some point in middle adolescence there occurs a cluster of spurts in optimal performance.

According to skill theory, similar spurts occur for each of the levels in Table 1 because of the emergence of the new optimal level. [Of course, other factors can produce spurts, too (Fischer and Bullock 1981)]. Consequently, optimal performance shows a series of clusters of spurts.

Yet ordinary performance under nonoptimal conditions is another matter entirely. Stages occur reliably only in optimal performance, not in ordinary performance. Usually behavior develops gradually and continuously, showing few sudden jumps. A major task for a theory of cognitive development in the real child is to depict the range of variations between optimal level and ordinary performance.

FUNCTIONAL LEVELS AND VARIATIONS IN ORDINARY PERFORMANCE

Most behavior involves variations below optimal level. Our research indicates that students rarely function at their optimum under the kinds of conditions that are used for assessment in the schools. Instead, they function at a level such as that suggested for the initial condition by the graph in Figure 1 (Session 1, No support). Adolescents seventeen or eighteen years of age, for example, failed the tasks requiring abstract mappings, passed some of the tasks for single abstractions, and passed virtually all the tasks for representational systems. Yet under optimal conditions they were clearly capable of abstract mappings. Their level of ordinary functioning was far below their level of optimal performance.

Indeed, our research has demonstrated a fragility in optimal performance in a number of domains. Without environmental support for high-level performance, behavior typically falls to a level far below the optimal. The findings in the arithmetic study were unusual in that students sustained much of their high level of performance in the no-support condition in

53

the second session. By hypothesis, that effect arose from the fact that these students were being taught mathematics regularly in high school, and so it was a highly familiar and practiced domain.

With the removal of support, children's performance levels in most domains plummet in a matter of minutes (Fischer and Elmendorf 1986; Lamborn and Fischer 1988). For example, when students between sixteen and twenty years of age were presented with a series of stories testing their understanding of the relations between intention and responsibility, many of them showed abstract mappings under optimal conditions. Ten minutes later, without the support of having just heard a story embodying a mapping, they were asked to present the best story they could about intention and responsibility. Their performance immediately plummeted. Not one student could sustain the optimal level of performance, even though he or she had done so just minutes before (Fischer, Hand, and Russell 1984).

Instead of performing at optimum, people seem ordinarily to perform at what is called their *functional level,* a limit on their functioning that is typically below what they can do under optimal conditions. Simple manipulations, such as instructing them to do the best they can or giving them the opportunity to practice, do not eliminate this gap between optimal and functional levels. They merely lead people to show their best possible spontaneous performance, their functional level. The only manipulation that seems consistently to reduce or eliminate the gap is reinstituting high environmental support, as was done in the arithmetic study.

One way of interpreting these findings is that people must internalize the high-level structure in order to be able to produce it without support. The high-support conditions show what they can understand when demands of internalization are minimal. The low-support conditions test whether they can produce and organize the complex skill on their own, whether they have internalized it. This process is related to what Vygotsky

(1978) referred to as learning in the zone of proximal development.

INDIVIDUAL DIFFERENCES
IN DEVELOPMENTAL PATHWAYS

Functional level describes only one way in which people show individual differences in development. According to skill theory, individual differences are the norm in development (Fischer and Elmendorf 1986), even while children also develop through the general levels in Table 1. The specific skills, and therefore the capacities or competencies, vary widely as a function of the children's experiences, their emotions and interests, and their special facilities or disabilities. Whenever possible, assessments of children's developing skills should allow the detection of different developmental sequences. However, many developmental studies are designed so that they cannot detect such individual differences (Fischer and Silvern 1985).

As they master early reading skills, for example, children follow several distinct pathways (Knight 1982; Knight and Fischer 1987). One of the primary tasks of reading is to integrate visual information, captured in writing and print, with sound information, used in normal spoken language. For example, the letters *t, r, e,* and *e* have to be integrated with the sounds in the word *tree*. There are, of course, a number of different potential tasks for assessing this integration. One of the major dimensions along which such tasks vary in our research is degree of environmental support for high-level performance. For example, a recognition task, which allows the child to match the written word with a picture of a tree, provides more support than a production task, which requires the child to produce the spoken word *tree* from the written word without any contextual support.

Figures 2 and 3 show developmental sequences for normal readers and those with sound-analysis deficiency. Each child shows the full sequence in one of the figures. Parallel lines indicate that the skills in the two lines are developing in each child in the order shown but are not related across lines.

In the normative sequence shown in Figure 2, children show separate development of some visual tasks, such as identifying written letters in words, and some sound tasks, such as recognizing rhymes for the same words. As children move down the sequence toward reading production (without environmental support), the visual and sound tasks come to order together because the visual and sound components have been integrated. Rhyming production and reading production thus develop in sequence.

In the sequence for the sound-analysis deficiency, shown in Figure 3, the visual and sound tasks do not come together. Instead, they continue to develop along separate lines in the child. This lack of integration of vision and sound seems to arise from a general deficiency in sound analysis skills (Bradley and Bryant 1983; Pennington et al. 1984). Indeed, most children with specific dyslexia seem to suffer from such sound-analysis problems. Thus dyslexia shows one primary developmental pattern, even though the deficiency appears to arise from diverse sources, ranging from a lack of practice of sound-analysis skills to a specific, genetically based deficiency in sound analysis.

When dyslexic children were tested with a scale designed to provide a direct test of the sequence in Figure 2, they did not merely show low-level performance. Their behavior did not fit the scale but, instead, fit the scale in Figure 3. With most reading assessments there have been no such strict tests of sequence. Without such tests dyslexic children would merely seem to be slow developmentally. Only with the direct test of the sequence has it been possible to determine that, unlike normal readers, these children showed a different developmental pattern.

Figure 2
Modal Developmental Sequence for Early Reading

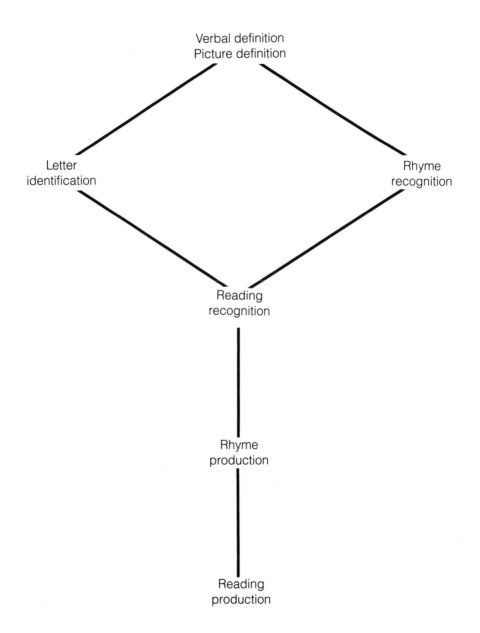

Figure 3
Developmental Sequence for Low Readers
(Read Better Than Rhyme)

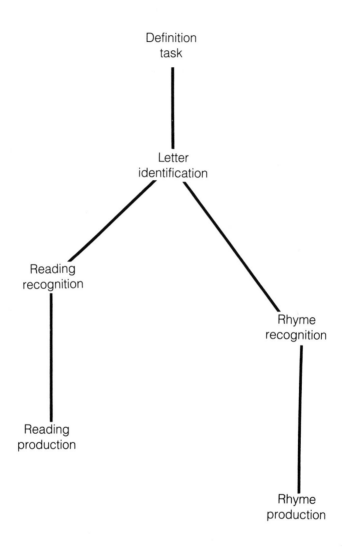

According to skill theory, children show many such individual differences in developmental sequences, but assessment methods often make it impossible to detect these differences. Research that allows such detection should uncover wide variations in developmental patterns.

APPLICATION TO ASSESSMENT OF REFLECTIVE JUDGMENT

One of the primary lessons from these several research findings is that both developmental sequences and variations should be directly assessed. That is, in any given domain an assessment should include both a range of tasks for assessing different developmental levels and a range of assessment conditions for assessing the developmental range between optimal and functional levels. Using such assessments, researchers can begin to describe both the sequences and the variations in the behavior of real children (Fischer and Canfield 1986). Then their theories of cognitive development will prove to be much more useful in working with real children.

Based on this rationale, several of us have been devising instruments for assessing development in various domains, including arithmetic concepts scales and reading skills scales. With regard to thinking skills, we should also mention a third assessment instrument—reflective judgment scales. A study in progress on these scales illustrates what can be expected in most areas that can be investigated with this sort of methodology.

With Kitchener we have developed a battery of tasks for assessing levels and variations in the development of the kind of higher-order thinking called *reflective judgment*. Kitchener and King (1981) formulated a theory of the development of understanding the bases for knowing that culminates in the conception of reflective judgment. Table 2 reflects the sequence of seven stages in this development, as well as Kitchener's (1982) analysis of how they relate to the levels of skill theory.

Table 2
Development of Reflective Judgment

Skill Level	Stage of Reflective Judgment
Rp 1: Single representations	Stage 1: Single category for knowing: To know means to observe directly without evaluation.
Rp 2: Representational mappings	Stage 2: Two categories for knowing: People can be right about what they know, or they can be wrong.
Rp 3: Representational systems	Stage 3: Three categories for knowing: People can be right about what they know, or they can be wrong, or knowledge might be incomplete or temporarily unavailable. The status of knowledge might differ in different areas.
Rp 4/A 1: Systems of representational systems, which are single abstractions	Stage 4: Knowledge is uncertain: The fact that knowledge is unknown in several instances leads to an initial understanding of knowledge as an abstract process that is uncertain.
A 2: Abstract mappings	Stage 5: Knowledge is relative to a context or viewpoint; it is subject to interpretation. Thus, it is uncertain in science, history, philosophy, etc. Conclusions must be justified. Abstract systems
A 3: Abstract systems	Stage 6: Although knowledge is uncertain and subject to interpretation, it is possible to abstract some justified conclusions across domains or viewpoint. Knowledge is an outcome of these processes.

Table 2 (Continued)

Skill Level	Stage of Reflective Judgment
A 4: Systems of abstract systems, which are principles	Stage 7 Knowledge occurs probabilistically via inquiry, which unifies concepts of knowledge.

Note: Stages are adapted from Kitchener and King's (1981) Reflective Judgment Scale.

In the early stages children show little reflectivity in their conception of knowing, thinking in terms of simple right and wrong. During the intermediate stages they come to understand the uncertainty of knowledge. Gradually at the higher stages they articulate such concepts as viewpoint, justification, and evidence. By the final stage, they understand that knowledge can be fairly certain, provided that it is based on a coherent viewpoint that considers evidence and provides justifications for a conclusion.

Kitchener and King's (1981) first instrument for assessing these stages used an interview based on dilemmas about knowledge (the Reflective Judgment Interview).

For example, students were asked to consider who built the Egyptian pyramids. Were the ancient Egyptians capable of building the pyramids on their own, or did they require some sort of aid from a more advanced civilization? Using four such dilemmas, Kitchener and King found in a longitudinal study that people did, in fact, move through the seven stages as predicted.

The Reflective Judgment Interview provides little environmental support for high-level performance. Kitchener and Fischer have devised a new instrument, the Prototypic Reflective Judgment Interview, by which people are assessed under high-support conditions. For each dilemma at each stage, they are given a prototypic answer and then asked to explain that answer.

In a study in progress subjects were first assessed with the low-support Reflective Judgment Interview. Second, they were given the high-support Prototypic Reflective Judgment Interview. Then, as in the arithmetic study, they were given two weeks to think about the dilemmas and assessed again.

We are predicting that the results will be more complex than in the arithmetic study because students are not regularly instructed on the bases of knowledge in the same way that they are instructed on arithmetic concepts. Consequently, students will show an optimal-level effect primarily when on their own they show interest in understanding the bases of knowledge. Most students will not reach their optimal level in this domain. Much more instruction would be required for them to attain the optimal performance level (Fischer and Lamborn 1989; Fischer and Farrar 1987).

The high-support assessment will produce an increase in stage, and this increase will consolidate during the second session. That is, students will show an increase in the consistency of their judgments in the second session. Nevertheless, spontaneous performance in the low-support condition will continue to be at a far lower functional level, thus demonstrating once again the gap between high-support and low-support performance. Skills are hard to learn and sustain, and in most domains performance will routinely occur below the optimal level, even with high-support assessments and the opportunity for practice. Movement to the optimal level, the upper limit on performance, requires sustained work at mastering and internalizing the skills.

SUMMARY

Theorists of cognitive development have suffered from tendencies to think dichotomously about children's development. As a result, their concepts have often failed to be helpful in educational practice. For example, one group has typically focused primarily on searching for stages to characterize the children and has neglected the role of task and environment. Another group has focused primarily on analyses of tasks and has neglected the contribution of the child.

Skill theory is designed to analyze the development of real children—children who vary in capacity, motivation, and emotional state and who act in specific contexts. The central constructs of this theory are defined in terms of both child and environmental variables. As a result, skill theory shows how real children can exhibit both stagelike developmental levels and wide variations in performance.

Development moves through a series of hierarchically organized cognitive levels, with seven levels identified between the ages of two and thirty. Each level produces a discontinuous spurt in capacity, but most behaviors do not reflect these spurts because the levels specify the upper limit on performance. These levels are evident only under optimal performance conditions—with familiar, well-practiced tasks; contextual support for high-level performance; and motivated, healthy children. Under those conditions, children demonstrate stagelike development of capacities in, for example, both understanding arithmetic concepts and describing their own personalities.

Most classroom behavior involves variations below the optimal level. Our research indicates that students rarely function at their optimum under the kinds of conditions that are used for assessment in the schools. Instead, as they become familiar with a domain of tasks, they show a functional level—a limit on their functioning that is typically below what they can do under optimal conditions.

Real children also use different approaches to a task and, as a result, move through different developmental pathways. In mastering early reading skills, for example, children show at least two distinct pathways. One pathway may be a much more frequent descriptor of at-risk students.

This theory applies as well as to the development of critical thinking skills. Kitchener and Fischer have developed a battery of tasks for assessing levels and variations in the development of reflective judgment, one kind of critical thinking. In contrast to the arithmetic study, which focused on skills being intensively taught in school, this assessment is expected to produce results more typical of domains that are not yet major targets of school instruction. Even with environmental support for high-level performance, many people will not demonstrate their optimal level because of variations in motivation and background experience. Some students will reach the upper limit in each age group, but others will reach a functional level across tasks that is below their optimum. In addition, the gap between high-support and low-support conditions will remain large for most learners.

REFERENCES

Bradley, L., and Bryant, P. E. 1983. Categorizing sounds and learning to read: A causal connection. *Nature* 301: 419–21.

Chi, M. T. H. 1978. Knowledge structures and memory development. In *Children's thinking: What develops?* ed. R. S. Siegler, 73–96. Hillsdale, N.J.: Lawrence Erlbaum Associates.

Colby, A.; Kohlberg, L.; Gibbs, J.; and Lieberman, M. 1983. *A longitudinal study of moral judgment.* Monographs of the Society for Research in Child Development, vol. 48, no. 1, serial no. 200.

Fischer, K. W. 1980. A theory of cognitive development: The control and construction of hierarchies of skills. *Psychological Review* 87: 477–531.

Fischer, K. W., and Bullock, D. 1981. Patterns of data: Sequence, synchrony, and constraint in cognitive development. In *Cognitive development*, ed. K. W. Fischer, 69–78. New Directions for Child Development, no. 12. San Francisco: Jossey-Bass.

Fischer, K. W., and Bullock D. 1984. Cognitive development in school-age children: Conclusions and new directions. In *The years from six to twelve: Cognitive development during middle childhood*, ed W. A. Collins, 70–146. Washington, D.C.: National Academy Press.

Fischer, K. W., and Canfield, R. L. 1986. The ambiguity of stage and structure in behavior: Person and environment in the development of psychological structures. In *Stage and structure*, ed. I. Levin, 246–67. New York: Plenum.

Fischer, K. W., and Elmendorf, D. 1986. Becoming a different person: Transformations in personality and social behavior. In *Minnesota symposia on child psychology*. Vol. 18, ed. M. Perlmutter 137–78. Hillsdale, N.J.: Lawrence Erlbaum Associates.

Fischer, K. W., and Farrar, M. J. 1987. Generalizations about generalization: How a theory of skill development explains both generality and specificity. *International Journal of Psychology* 22: 643–77.

Fischer, K. W.; Hand, H. H.; and Russell, S. L. 1984. The development of abstractions in adolescence and adulthood. In *Beyond formal operations*, ed. M. Commons, F. A. Richards, and C. Armon, 43–73. New York: Praeger.

Fischer, K. W., and Kenny, S. L. 1986. The environmental conditions for discontinuities in the development of abstractions. In *Adult cognitive development: methods and models*, ed. R. Mines and K. Kitchener, 57–75. New York: Praeger.

Fischer, K. W., and Lamborn, S. 1989. Sources of variations in developmental levels: Cognitive and emotional transitions during adolescence. In *Mechanisms of transition in cognitive and emotional development*, ed. A. de Ribaupierre. New York: Cambridge University Press.

Fischer, K. W., and Pipp, S. L. 1984. Processes of cognitive development: Optimal level and skill acquisition. In *Mechanisms of cognitive development*, ed. R. J. Sternberg, 45–80. New York: W. H. Freeman & Co.

Fischer, K. W.; Pipp, S. L.; and Bullock, D. 1984. Detecting developmental discontinuities; methods and measurement. In *Continuities and discontinuities in development*, ed. R. Emde and R. Harmon, 95–121. New York: Plenum.

Fischer, K. W., and Silvern, L. 1985. Stages and individual differences in cognitive development. *Annual Review of Psychology* 36: 613–48.

Harter, S. 1986. Cognitive-developmental processes in the integration of concepts about emotions and the self. *Social Cognition* 4: 119–51.

Kitchener, K. S. 1982. Human development and the college campus: Sequences and tasks. In *Measuring student development*, ed. G. R. Hanson, 17–45. New Directions for Student Services, no. 20. San Francisco: Jossey-Bass.

Kitchener, K. S., and King, P. M. 1981. Reflective judgment: Concepts of justification and their relation to age and education. *Journal of Applied Developmental Psychology* 2: 89–116.

Klahr, D., and Wallace, J. G. 1976. *Cognitive development: An information-processing review.* Hillsdale, N.J.: Lawrence Erlbaum Associates.

Knight, C. C. 1982. Hierarchical relationships among components of reading abilities of beginning readers. Ph.D. diss. Arizona State University, Tempe.

Knight, C. C., and Fischer, K. W. 1987. Learning to read: Patterns of skill development and individual differences. Typescript.

Kohlberg, L. 1969. Stage and sequence: The cognitive developmental approach to socialization. In *Handbook of socialization theory and research*, ed. D. A. Goslin, 347–480. Chicago: Rand McNally.

Lamborn, S. D. 1987. *Relations between social-cognitive knowledge and personal experience: Understanding honesty and kindness in relationships.* Ann Arbor, Mich.: University Microfilms.

Lamborn, S. D., and Fischer, K. W. 1988. Optimal and functional levels in cognitive development: The individual's developmental range. *Newsletter of the International Society for the Study of Behavioral Development* 2 (serial no. 14): 1–4.

Monsour, A. 1985. *The dynamics and structure of adolescent self-concept.* Ann Arbor, Mich.: University Microfilms.

Pennington, G.; Smith, S.; McCabe, L.; Kimberling, W.; and Lubs, H. 1984. Developmental continuities and discontinuities in a form of familial dyslexia. In *Continuities and discontinuities in development*, ed. R. Emde and R. Harmon. New York: Plenum.

Piaget, J. 1971. The theory of stages in cognitive development. In *Measurement and Piaget*, ed. D. R. Green, M. P. Ford, and G. B. Flamer. New York: McGraw-Hill.

Piaget, J. 1983. Piaget's theory. In *Handbook of child psychology.* 4th ed., ed. P. H. Mussen. Vol. 1, *History, theory, and methods,* ed. W. Kessen, 103–26. New York: John Wiley.

Siegler, R. S. 1983. Information processing approaches to development. In *Handbook of child psychology.* 4th ed., ed. P. H. Mussen. Vol. 1, *History, theory, and methods,* ed. W. Kessen, 129–211. New York: John Wiley.

Vygotsky, L. 1978. *Mind in society: The development of higher psychological processes.* Trans. M. Cole, V. John-Steiner, S. Scribner, and Ellen Souberman. Cambridge, Mass.: Harvard University Press.

Chapter 4

THE THEORY OF STRUCTURAL COGNITIVE MODIFIABILITY

by Reuven Feuerstein

The need to organize data, observations, and interpretations into an all-embracing theory is consistent with the need of scientists to be guided both in their research and in the interpretations of their findings by a comprehensive whole. A theory thus serves as a guideline and a selecting, organizing principle that engenders relationships that would otherwise escape in a multitude of details. In certain cases, if these relationships are not perceived, or if they are reduced to randomized appearances, inconsistencies and incompatibilities would be created. The law of parsimony in science seeks to explain phenomena as economically as possible. A theory has a similar goal and must be applied with caution and a certain degree of suspicion. There must be compatibility between the economy of assumptions in reasoning, or the ascriptions of existence that emerge from the law of parsimony, and the multitude of diverse phenomena with which a theory attempts to deal. A theory that attempts to address the relationships between intelligence and children's ability to think is no less constrained.

In the following pages we will outline the critical elements of a theory of intelligence. In reviewing the various theories that have been proposed in the past, we find that many of them deal only partially with those components we consider to be the most important. Let us consider these components.

First, most essential of the components of a theory of intelligence is that its subject be well defined. The answer to the question, "What is intelligence?" will certainly affect the theory's course of development in terms of its organization, its content, and its meaning.

Second, the theory must deal with the origin of the object of concern, "How does intelligence come into being?"

A third issue to be addressed in a theory of intelligence is concerned with the conditions that prevent this particular object from coming into being. Thus the question develops, "What will make the existence of intelligence differ widely in the modalities of its appearance and in its qualitative and quantitative dimensions?"

A fourth question of concern to a theory of intelligence is, "What is the nature of intelligence in terms of its stability/modifiability?"

A fifth element of the theory is the meaning of intelligence in the total of human behavior.

A sixth component addresses the diversification of intelligence and outlines the determinants of this diversification.

A seventh issue that must be addressed is the most appropriate methodology by which to operationalize some of the mental constructs that are used as building blocks in the construction of the theory of intelligence.

Finally, an eighth concern: if we opt for an interactional approach to intelligence, and declare intelligence to be a process rather than a reified object (with the process defined as a constant progression toward higher levels of adaptation), then we must ask, "What is it that enhances the occurrence of such processes, and, to the contrary, what are the conditions whose presence or absence are barriers to the processes of adaptation?"

We will attempt to describe the theory of Structural Cognitive Modifiability by responding selectively to several of the various questions posed. We consider it neither possible nor appropriate to enter into a detailed discussion of all the factors, but we hope that in addressing a significant group, an initial outline of a theory of intelligence will emerge. Other theories of intelligence will be discussed and confronted, but only to the extent necessary in order to better present and delimit the borders of the theory we propose.

DEFINITION OF TERMS

As we suggested, the definition of intelligence is a very important component of its theory. We will not attempt to review the various definitions familiar to the reader from the literature. However, we would like to remind the reader of the recent judicious attempts in which the term is not only considered globally, but as a conglomerate of diverse factors that may appear differentially in individuals, as well as in various groups.

The triarchic concept of intelligence proposed and elaborated by Robert Sternberg (1985), Howard Gardner's hypothesis of the multiple forms of intelligence (1983), and the factorial description of intelligence by a number of other authors—all address the way the basic definition is manifested differentially in individuals and groups. They also discuss how these diverse manifestations are linked to specific situations. Thus, in his beautiful metaphorical representation of mental life as a governmental system, Sternberg's basic definition refers to intelligence as the faculty by which the organism adapts to novel situations. The concept of novel or more complex situations is a sine qua non, since it is inherent in a concept of adaptation. The triarchic theory of intelligence describes the diverse and specific modalities and the personal styles of individuals whose cognitive structure—with its cognitive, emotional, and experiential deter-minants—is oriented toward preferential modalities of adapta-tion. Thus, the common underlying concept in the definition of intelligence in Sternberg's theory is the process of *adaptation.* Various authors have conceptualized the process in certain modalities, grouping and categorizing manifestations of intelligence in relation to certain situations and life conditions (Sternberg and Detterman 1986).

At this point in our search for a definition of intelligence in order to construct a theory, we contend that *intelligence should be defined as a process broad enough to embrace a large variety of phenomena that have in common the dynamics and mechanics of adaptation.* It is adaptability that is inherent in both problem solving, which reflects purely cognitive elements, and creativity, which is engendered by strong motivational elements. It may even be necessary to redefine the concept of adaptability to render it broad enough to define intelligence. Philosophically and morally, adaptability is usually described as overtly serving an organism's positive goal for survival, the survival of others, and the preservation of certain states of mind. In our broadening of the concept, however, we may reject the positive nature of adaptation as its sole criterion. If so, nothing—neither biologically based needs nor emotional, moral, or philosophical orientations—may preclude the application of the concept of adaptability, once we admit the possibility of including in the forces of adaptation those behaviors leading to outcomes imcompatible with the usual goals of adaptation, such as survival. Negative outcomes may, under specific conditions, capacities, and behavior, actually reflect adaptation.

It is, therefore, adaptation in it most generic term that we advocate: the changes that the organism undergoes in response to the appearance of a novel situation that requires such changes in the organism. It is a *dynamic process* that represents a more-or-less consciously, more-or-less volitionally, engendered process of change from one state to another. It is this adaptability of the organism (the individual or the group) that we refer to as *modifiability.* That this modifiability may differ from individual to individual, from state to state, from situation to situation, is a phenomenon that is too often observed to need further elaboration.

For example, differences are observed between normal and autistic children in their heart rate change following their adaptation to a new situation. Following exposure to a particular set of stimuli that has produced changes in state of alertness, galvanic skin response (GSR), respiratory system and heartbeat, habituation in a normal child is manifested by a decrease and regularization of these neurovegetative phenomena. The autistic child shows neither these changes nor habituation when presented with such stimuli. In some cases, there is not even the expected arousal. In other words, the rate of change may vary greatly even in such elementary phenomena, and even more in molar conditions of exposure to situations requiring adaptation. The origin of this differential rate of adaptability and diversity in the process of change must therefore be questioned.

ORIGIN OF DIVERSITY IN RATE OF ADAPTABILITY

One way we identify individuals with a wide array of deficient functions is by their slow and limited modifiability, or even its absence. Rather than describing a person as a member of a category labeled "retarded" or "high-level gifted," etc., we prefer to describe these individual differences in terms of the process or the dynamics of change: the rate and quality of change; the nature, frequency, and intensity of the stimuli required to produce the given change as a structural characteristic of an individual. (Structural, because it relates to a nucleal determinant responsible for variations in a highly diverse universe of behaviors.)

Modifiability need not be similar in all areas. This characteristic of the process of change may display variations. It is this very nature of the individual's modifiability that is responsible for the manifestation of deficiencies, as well as for the rapid modifiability that is evidenced through higher levels of functioning. It no longer sounds contradictory, once we sharply distinguish between manifest level of functioning and the latent behavior revealed in the process of change.

The definition of intelligence as a process rather than a reified, immutable, fixed entity thus carries with it some dramatic differences in the way behaviors are perceived. In describing the dynamics of this process, we must take into account other elements responsible for the adaptability in the individual's behavior. These components, whether they be emotional or cognitive, will have to be revealed. The role they play in the nature and process of change will have to be analyzed, understood, and eventually given a particular weight.

If we accept this definition of intelligence as a process rather than as a reified object, with all that entails both theoretically and empirically, we must investigate the notion of the origin of intelligence as having an adaptive meaning. How does this interpretation influence the individual? Through its propensity to integrate into previously formed schemata the learning derived from new experiences, previous schemata are modified so as to make them adaptable to the new situation that has been produced through the new experience. In a sense, the Piagetian concept of assimilation and accommodation is highly consonant with the view of intelligence as a process and as a nonreified entity (Piaget 1970). The plasticity of the schemata that permits assimilation to end by changing the schemata, which is accommodating to the new stimuli, information, and experience, represents a dynamic view of intelligence as a process.

If this view is accepted, what then is the origin of the flexibility, the plasticity and modifiability of those schemata that are changed by experience so as to adapt to new experiences? It is agreed that instinct—with its inborn schemata—does not show this kind of flexibility. On the contrary, instinct and reflex behavior are defined as unidirectional and nonmodifiable entities. In its confrontation with experience, instinctive behavior does not modify its inborn course of functioning. Nor is the perceptual process, as described by Piaget, flexible enough to deserve the term intelligence. In contradistinction to intelligence, in our view, perceptual processes can be modified only through a cognitive approach, with "the cognitive crutches" helping "the limping perception" to adapt to new situations.

We know that modifiability is a process that differentiates meaningfully among human beings and thereby reflects the different degree of their manifest adaptation. Many of the difficulties people have in academic areas, in particular, and in life in general, for instance, are due to a limited, poor, or nonexistent capacity to benefit from formal or informal learning situations. When we speak of learning disabilities—which may be circumscribed to one particular area or one particular mode of functioning—we are describing the incapacity of an individual to benefit or become modified through exposure to certain experiences that are effected with other people. What is it that makes one organism more or less able to benefit from experience? May we call these people more or less intelligent? What actually forms a barrier to plasticity, flexibility, and modifiability? The answer is very difficult because of the manifold sources and origins of these differences. In terms of a theory, however, we suggest that differences are due not only to the nature of the organism, which they certainly are, but also to a typical human mode of interacting with the world, which affects precisely this quality of the human experience.

If we compare animal intelligence to human intelligence, we see that the degree of modifiability ascribed to and observed in humanoid forms of life is extremely limited. Even in the case of the anthropoid, the area and extent of change that can be anticipated is minimal. In their natural life, when animals respond and eventually even adapt, their adaptation has a very limited range. Rather than changing themselves, animals often change environments. They learn to look for elements that correspond to the schemata at their disposal and make the best use of them. This is in contradistinction to humans, whose environment includes a motivating mediator intent on making them learn a specific behavior. Under these circumstances, their learning capacity becomes meaningfully increased; it reaches levels of functioning not easily found when they are left to themselves and are directly confronted with situations and stimuli. It is the quality of interaction with a motivating, intentioned mediator that animals lack, despite the repertoire of schemata of their natural life.

Given the above distinction, we may compare the two modalities by which the human organism is modified with the single modality of change of an animal. The one pervasive modality, the direct exposure to stimuli, is indeed a source of change for both humans and animals. It ensures a certain mode of adaptation, limited both in its scope and in its nature, which we refer to as "one-to-one correspondence." A situation appears; there is some change in behavior in order to adapt to the particularity of the situation. With this, the adaptation process is finished. Another situation will be required for the same adaptation to result. Direct exposure is certainly responsible for many of the types of changes produced in humans. However, it is the second modality of interaction between the human and the environment, the Mediated Learning Experience (MLE), that is responsible for a more meaningful and generalized type of change that actually assumes a structural nature. It does not require a repetition of the same sequence of steps by which adaptation took place initially.

Thus, MLE is an interaction during which the human organism is subject to the intervention of a mediator. Learners can benefit not only from the direct exposure to a particular stimulus, but they can also forge in themselves a repertoire of dispositions, propensities, orientations, attitudes, and techniques that enable them to modify themselves in relation to other stimuli. Our hypothesis, then, is that MLE is the determinant responsible for the development of the flexibility of the schemata which ensures that the stimuli that impinge on us will affect us in a meaningful way. MLE produces the plasticity and flexibility of adaptation that we call intelligence.

The ontogeny of this unique and specifically human characteristic cannot simply be explained by the individual's maturational process. Individual differences in the rate of learning can be observed at an early age. Piaget himself described differences in the onset of eye-hand coordination among his own three children. He does not ascribe these differences to variations in the children's rate of maturation, but rather to the various amount of exercises that had been offered to each. We would refer to this as the frequency and intensity of MLE interactions.

Through mediated intervention, the author has succeeded in making his eight-week-old Down's syndrome grandchild repeat clearly the lip movements related to "bu" and "ba," with appropriate facial kinesis. What is more important, however, is the change in the infant's rate of learning in response to mediation observed over time. Eliciting a behavior lacking from the baby's repertoire had previously taken about 200 repetitions; now only ten repeated exposures are necessary to elicit a new behavior. The change produced by MLE has not only been in the realm of learned content, but in the learning structure, in the propensity for learning, and in the growing capacity of the organism (the infant in this particular case) to benefit from exposure to learning situations.

When we compare the amount and nature of exposure needed by the baby's eighteen-month-old sister, the same change has been produced in the little girl with far less investment. We therefore recognize that variations in the investment necessary to produce the plasticity and modifiability of individuals, reflected in the differential rate of their learning process, are grounded in variations in the organism's innate conditions. These variations may have a neurochemical, neurophysiological origin that, indeed, may vary from individual to individual. But must these variations be considered as inevitably leading to gross differences between the level of functioning of individuals? Is it not possible to conceive of variations in intervention that may overcome initial differences partially, but meaningfully?*

Another reason that changes in the rate of learning-intelligence should not be attributed to maturation is that the rate of development is not uniform even when *toute chose est egal d'ailleur*, when all conditions seem to be equal for all individuals. In dealing with the maturation-environment interaction, Piaget has given little, if any, consideration to the great differences among individuals in the development of those cognitive processes that he considered to be the universal outcome of the maturation-environment interaction. How many of those who attain the age of formal operations also attain the operations themselves? The author has confronted Piaget with data that prove that groups of North African children and young adults functioned on the level of five to six year olds in Geneva in operational areas, despite their normal development and level of functioning in most other areas. The North African population had clearly not attained the level of operational thinking, despite their age and their rich opportunity to interact directly with stimuli, the Piagetian formula of development of intelligence/content. The Piagetian concept of Stimulus-Organism-Response (S-O-R) does not really explain differential development, as presented in Sternberg's triarchic theory or in the multifaceted approach of Gardner and others (Sternberg 1985; Gardner 1983).

In an article on the first humans that recently appeared in *U.S. News and World Report*, William F. Allman concludes:

> Thus, merely having a larger brain may not have been enough to produce the maturation rate seen in modern humans. That came only later, perhaps when parents had more time to care for children because of an abundance of food, possibly due to the development of regular hunting for large game. (p. 58)

---

*See recent research of R. A. Leemann on brain formation and thinking.

It therefore seems to us that the simple maturational or even interactional hypothesis of S-O-R is unable to explain the plasticity of the human organism. We recognize the importance of the Baldwin-Piagetian concept of assimilation, accommodation, and equilibration in describing the dynamics of change in human sensorimotor, concrete, and later formal operations. Our question is, what makes the schemata flexible enough to allow this process to occur and what is it that precludes this process from taking place in certain individuals? The human's modifiability under a variety of conditions, its functioning through hierarchically higher modalities of operation, and its considerable diversification in its interactions under diverse situations must be explained. Our theoretically derived stance is that what makes both the innate and acquired schemata plastic and modifiable is the second modality of human-environment interaction, namely MLE.

MLE INTERACTIONS

MLE is defined as a quality of human-environment interaction that results from the changes introduced in this interaction by a human mediator who interposes him/herself between the receiving organism and the sources of stimuli. The mediator selects, organizes, and schedules the stimuli, changing their amplitude, frequency and saliency; and turns them into powerful determinants of behavior instead of randomized stimuli whose occurrence, registration, and effects may be purely probabilistic. Animated by an intention to make a chosen stimulus available to the mediatee, the mediator is not content with its random presentation but will rather meaningfully change the three components of the mediated interaction: the receiving organism (the mediatee), the stimulus, and the mediator him/herself. Thus, when the author attempted to mediate the facial kinetics related to the sounds "bu," "ba," he amplified his lip movements so they became visible to the fleeting sight of the infant, repeated the sounds numerous times, modulated his voice so as to make it less monotonous, ensured that the infant focused on him as a model by adapting his position to the position of the baby or by holding the baby in the position most conducive for the registration of changes in the mediator's behavior. Thus the mediator's intention to make a particular stimuli available to the mediatee meaningfully changes the stimulus from a fleeting, randomized, almost imperceptible occurrence to a powerful, inescapable encounter that will be registered, integrated, and mastered by the learner.

As previously described, however, the major and unique effect of MLE is not the acquisition of the mediated specific stimulus. This may also happen under specified optimal conditions of direct and nonmediated accidental exposure to the same stimulus. The unique effect of MLE is the creation in the mediatees (whether they be infants, children, adolescents, or adults) of a disposition, an attitudinal propensity to benefit from the direct exposure to stimuli. Ways are created to focus not only on the stimulus, but also on the relationships of proximity-distance, of temporal and spatial order, of the constancy-transformation complex, and on a variety of higher-order perceptions and elaborations of the stimuli. Thus, there is an increasing expansion of the schemata from their pure sensorimotor or perceptual nature to their abstract level of formal mental operations. This transition, described by Piaget, cannot be considered simply as the epiphenomenon of our direct exposure to stimuli, nor even of our active interaction with them. It requires the active interposition of the mediator whose intentions are marked by a goal that transcends by far the immediacy of the interaction. Without the dimensions of intentionality and transcendence, the acquired stimuli would have little meaning beyond what they represent. They would remain an episode with limited links to a larger category of events. It is the MLE that ultimately ensures that direct exposure to stimuli, the more universal modality of our interaction with the surrounding world, will become a source of change of structural nature. The repertoire of the individual's mental activity will thus be enriched with new structures of behaviors that were previously nonexistent in his/her active or even passive repertoire.

In the last proposition, we refer to the Vygotskian theory that conceives of the impact of social mediation as facilitating the passage from the current level of functioning to the level included in the "zone of proximal development" (Vygotsky 1962). Vygotsky implies that facilitation is related to a latent type of functioning that may eventually be reached without the intervention that has facilitated and antedated its appearance. Our contention, however, is that new cognitive structures are produced in the individual that would never come into being were it not for MLE and its role in their appearance. Indeed, more individuals in our world do *not* reach higher-order thinking skills than those who do. The reader is referred to the large literature on MLE for further elaboration of this subject. For the purposes of this chapter, however, and to discuss the origin of the construct of intelligence, which we have defined as the plasticity and flexibility that lead to the ever-expansion of schemata, we will briefly describe some of the characteristics of MLE.

CHARACTERISTICS OF MLE

The quality of the MLE interaction that is responsible for the formation and development of modifiability is ensured by the three parameters: intentionality, transcendence, and meaning. These are universally pervasive and omnipresent qualities in all human mediated interactions. They are common for all cultures, irrespective of their level of technology, or level and modality of communication. The three parameters have animated mothers and fathers since the onset of humanity, probably even preceding it since they are actually responsible for its development. MLE is the modality of interaction, irrespective of its content or the language in which it is carried out. Intentionality, transcendence, and the mediation of meaning ensure the formation of the flexible schemata and the ensuing modifiability that is the common trait of humanity. The other parameters of MLE are situationally determined or belong to the cultural norms of the group or the family. They may or may not be present in any MLE interaction. They are responsible for the diversification of humans, both as cultural groups and as individuals in the group.

In this way, we may speak of two aspects of human intelligence. The common and unique trait is the human modifiability and plasticity that lead us to the postulate that modifiability is accessible to all human beings, irrespective of the exogenous or endogenous etiology of their condition, their age, and the severity of their condition. The other aspect of humanity is obviously its considerable capacity to diversify itself in some critical aspects of its mental behavior, cognitive style, and modality of interaction. For example, the extent to which a culture develops an autonomous regulation of behavior differs widely in accordance with the conditions in which this culture lives and its view of the adaptive meaning of regulation of behavior, which may differ from culture to culture. Similarly, there is a great difference in the amount and strength of the feeling of competence a given culture or an intentioned mother mediates to the child. There are cultures that do not promote or encourage a feeling of individual competence. In Jewish culture, the origin of competence is ascribed to G-d, from whom the group or other figures of the family may derive their competence. A typical manifestation of this attitude is a kind of reverse plagiarism. Jewish literature is replete with writings of Jewish scholars who attribute their own writings to an illustrious image, preferably someone venerated in past ages and, of course, dead. Another example is sharing behavior, which is neither a universal practice, nor is necessarily mediated either by parents or by the cultural agents responsible for the transmission of the values of the culture. Intercultural diversity is paralleled, too, by an intracultural diversification due to personalized styles and preferences, which may play important roles in the formation of styles.

As previously stated, direct exposure to stimuli and MLE represent the two modalities of human-environment interactions that explain differential cognitive development. It is MLE, however, that should be considered the factor responsible for the individual's propensity to benefit from direct exposure, since it is through MLE that both the major components of learning and the modes of generalizing what is learned are established.

The theory of MLE that explains both the universality and diversity of human behavior should be contrasted with the behavioristic view of cognitive development (Stimulus-Response), and the Piagetian genetic theory (Stimulus-Organism-Response), which introduces the organism as a determinant. By the biological age-related level of its maturation and its active interaction with both the stimulus and response, the presence of the organism alters the nature of both the stimulus and response. The Piagetian model conceives of development as proceeding in a series of successive well-ordered stages. Each stage follows the other, capitalizing on the presence of the earlier stage to build a repertoire of functions that will compose the stage that will come next. It is analogous to the development of a monocotyledon plant whose leaves grow directly from its rootlets and appear successively in a well-determined order to form the stem. There is neither an enlargement nor branching of the physiologically determined stem. Instead, the leaves repeat themselves rhythmically and monotonously along the axis of the plant. The growth of the plant is highly predictable with little, if any, diversification in its critical aspects.

Direct exposure to stimuli as the only source of development of cognitive processes may be considered analogous to the development of the monocotyledon. Development is ordered along a hierarchical axis and follows the succession of growth imposed by this axis. It is thus universal, predictable, and totally independent of any culturally determined differences. There is neither a place for meaningful changes in the individual's level of functioning, nor is there a possibility of diversification or of structural modifiability.

The dicotyledon plant, on the other hand, is marked by a very different structure of growth. Its central root leads to a central stem; both the root and the stem develop powerful branches that form strong contacts with their environment and are highly affected by the natural conditions of the stimuli they encounter. For example, to a large extent the nature of the soil in which the roots develop determines many of the plant's structural qualities. It is impossible to predict the nature, quantity, and quality of growth of the dicotyledon simply by looking at its current growth pattern; one must also take into account its plasticity and modifiability in response to the variations of its growth environment. The branching of its roots is isomorphic and there is great diversity in the directions in which its branches grow. Contact with an undefined number of environmental conditions makes diversification and structural modifiability highly probable. On a metaphorical level, one is reminded of the process of arborization of the central nervous system, which is held responsible for the higher mental processes by increasing the contacts between the nerve cells, the formation of the cell assemblies, permitting interactions, exchanges, and combinations of information, and the subsequent changes in the mental processes toward hierarchically higher, more elaborate forms of abstract and conceptual thinking (Hebb 1949; Hunt 1961).

Notwithstanding the limitations of the analogy, the similarities are striking. The rich, powerful, and diverse influence of MLE on the cognitive, emotional, and personal development of the individual is the basis of modifiability, unpredictability, and the diversification of cognitive structure styles and need systems. The Garrett hypothesis, which postulated the progressive differentiation of intelligence with age, may be explained as a function of MLE that, through the transmission of culture over the years, offers the growing child a large variety of modes of thinking, of principles for organizing incoming data, of ways of educing relationships and using past experience to anticipate, plan, and shape the future (Garrett, Bryan, and Perl 1935).

Thus MLE fulfills two major roles. The first, its explanatory role, has been amply discussed in this chapter. Its second role is to serve as a guideline for shaping interactions that will produce the modifiability and flexibility so crucial to human adaptation and ultimately to survival.

MLE as a theory and applied system is more important today than ever before, not only because adaptability is required more, but also because of the current decrease of MLE as the pervasive modality of inter- and intragenerational interactions. There is now more attention to mass media than to personal address. Education and socialization have become delegated to professional agents whose emotional attachment to a particular child is of a more general nature and, unfortunately, often lacks the quality of the interactions between parents and children.

Many other socioeconomic, familial, and cultural conditions are at work in reducing the amount and quality of parental mediated interactions: the overreliance on the fragile structure of the nuclear family; the decrease in the numbers of enlarged families; the considerable increase in the number of single parents and working mothers; the growing pathology among parents that makes them disinterested in their children's quality of life presently and in the future. The millions of abandoned children in the world provide powerful testimony to what happens when parents and society are no longer animated by the need to shape their progeny by transmitting to them the past and the cultural values that have shaped them. The need to increase MLE in the normal population is no less than the need to provide MLE to a population whose endogenous conditions require a particular form of interaction to achieve its goal. MLE, because of its emphasis on the "how" of the interaction, irrespective of its "what" or the "language" it is expressed in, is particularly appropriate as a guideline for parents, teachers, and caregivers of all ethnocultural, socioeconomic, educational, and occupational levels.

EFFECTS OF MLE AND ITS ABSENCE

The hypothesis of the dual source of the development of intelligence now leads to the next question with which a theory of intelligence must deal: What are the effects of MLE and how will the lack of MLE affect an individual? The answer is not simple. Yet one can formulate the relationship between MLE and other modalities of learning: the more appropriate the MLE (in relating to the needs of the individual, which vary in terms of age as well as in particular neurophysiological and emotional conditions), the greater will be that individual's capacity to become modified through direct, autonomous exposure to stimuli. Inversely, the less MLE, the less modifiable the individual will be. This is true even for people who, by virtue of their psychophysical constitutions, are good and rapid learners. Without appropriate MLE, they may be deprived of some of the characteristics of human learning responsible for adaptability to new situations. This is the case, for instance, of gifted underachievers. They are certainly endowed with rapid perceptual and mental processing; however, devoid of MLE, they may be limited to certain types of incidental learning that are of little help in situations that demand systematic, laborious, selective, goal-oriented learning. The child at developmental risk cannot make much of the world of impinging stimuli without having prerequisites of learning established through MLE.

A few of the effects of MLE include imitative behavior, focusing, systematic search for relevant data, reevocation and retrieval of stored information, comparative behavior, and the use of one or more sources of information. In the mediation of the use of analogical thinking to transfer relationships from one set of data to another, similar in certain aspects, are the functions necessary for the generalization of acquired knowledge, principles, and relationships by transferring them to the other parts of the universe of content and operations. These operations, mediated to the individual through diverse contents, in a variety of languages and modalities of communication, render individuals modifiable by producing in them those prerequisite propensities, orientations, and attitudes that will enable them to generate new information.

Our response to the question of the determinant of intelligence (defined as plasticity) can be summarized by pointing to MLE, along with certain other characteristics of human beings and of individuals. A lack of MLE is manifested by the quasi-total absence, poor or reduced propensity for learning, and, ipso facto, of modifiability. Indeed one of the most commonly observed characteristics of those deprived of MLE for either exogenous or endogenous reasons, is a lack of modifiability in response to direct interactions with experienced stimuli and events.

STABILITY-MODIFIABILITY OF INTELLIGENCE

The fourth question concerning the stability-modifiability of intelligence finds its answer in what has preceded. MLE is a potent tool for the creation of flexibility and modifiability across conditions, age, stages of development, and the degree of severity of the individual's condition.

PROXIMAL AND DISTAL DETERMINANTS
OF COGNITIVE DEVELOPMENT

Differential cognitive development may be attributed to two distinct etiologies: a distal or proximal factor. Maturation, organicity, emotional and educational levels of parents and/or children, etc., are considered distal factors, since they neither necessarily nor unavoidably result in differential cognitive development. It is the second etiological factor, the proximal determinant, that we consider to be directly and inevitably responsible for both differential cognitive development and the degree of the modifiability typical for an individual. Distal determinants act as triggers for secondary processes referred to as the proximal determinants. The proximal determinant of utmost importance is the mediated learning experience. This conception of MLE as the proximal determinant of cognitive development, irrespective of any distal etiology, is illustrated in Figure 1.

Endogenous or exogenous distal factors may account for the lack of MLE. This lack may stem from internal factors set by an individual's endogenous condition, such as a genetic or chromosomal aberration, a centrally determined hyperactivity, sensory deprivation, or other types of deficiencies. Thus, for example, because of the child's hyperactive and hyperkinetic mode of interacting with the world or his/her hypoactive lowered sensitivity to general characteristics of the stimuli, or some specific critical elements, the child with an attention deficit may have great difficulties in attending to the mediator's efforts in selecting the stimulus and making the child focus on it.

Indeed, if the differences between retrospective and prospective research are considered, one becomes aware immediately that factors that had previously been considered determinants of human cognitive development based on retrospective research data proved to have limited meaning once the same phenomena were studied prospectively (see Sameroff and Chandler 1975). Thus, when looking retrospectively at the history of the child's dysfunction, one usually finds either a genetic or organic etiology at a pre-, para-, or postnatal level (i.e., the mother's condition during pregnancy; the process of the infant's delivery; or some postnatal adverse condition of physical, nutritional, emotional, or educational nature), which is described as being responsible, either in part or *in toto*, for the child's dysfunctioning. However, when the development of children who have undergone identical birth conditions is studied, one finds a very limited correlation with specific dysfunctions. The very interesting work of Pnina Klein (Klein and Feuerstein 1985) shows that the predictability of very low birth weight for future dysfunction is extremely limited when one takes into account educational and environmental factors, and more specifically, the presence or absence of MLE.

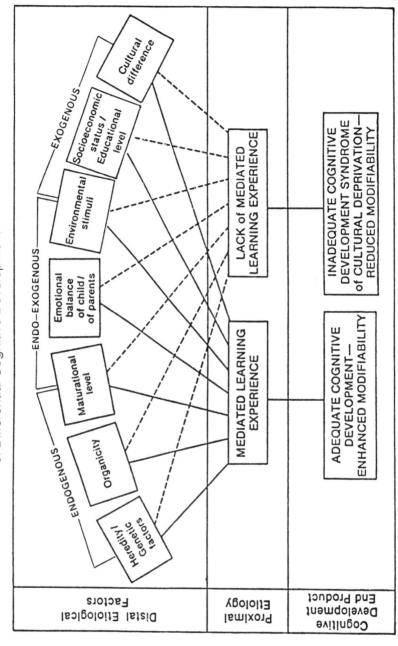

Figure 1
Distal and Proximal Determinants
of Differential Cognitive Development

Reading disabilities, for example, may be triggered by a particular distal determinant, such as minimal brain dysfunction (MBD), delayed development, perceptual inacuity of sensorial origin, lack of focusing, or any number of other factors. However, when we ask ourselves if all individuals suffering from similar conditions become dyslexic, the answer will be no. One person may remain unable to read, while another can learn to read with relative ease, despite his/her condition.

The author remembers, at the age of eight, that he was asked to coach in reading a fifteen-year-old reputedly "mentally retarded" adolescent. All previous attempts to help the boy read had failed and the specialized adult teachers had declared him to be totally unable to acquire reading or any other symbolic substitute of reality. His language was extremely poor and ungrammatical. The boy's father had half jokingly declared, "I'm not going to die unless my son is able to read the prayers at my death like a good Jewish boy." Indeed, animated by this powerful need, both the eight-year-old teacher and his student worked very hard to find ways to overcome the older boy's difficulties, resulting in his acquisition of reading skills. The adolescent's success affected the quality of his life. He developed subsequently much more normally and, despite lack of formal schooling, as an adult has become fully integrated into society. (He is now 75!) Motivation generated by a culturally determined need system and the resulting proximal MLE succeeded in bypassing and overcoming the barriers that were produced by some distal determinants.

The power of the proximal determinants, i.e., MLE in the acquisition of reading ability, is illustrated by the children from Yemen. The author personally met hundreds of Yemenite children and adolescents as they arrived in Israel from Yemen in the mid-1940s. Having met children from other cultures—Rumanian, Polish, Hungarian, Indian, Iraqi, and North African—he observed that one outstanding characteristic that distinguished the Yemenites from other groups was the total literacy in both reading and speech that was typical of the entire population from very young ages. Considering the technical difficulties this group had in obtaining books to read, how did this pervasive literacy happen? The Yemenite children had learned to read in all directions: left to right, upside down, right to left, and even diagonally because a whole group would read simultaneously from one book placed in the center, and each individual had to read from wherever he/she was. Their high motivation and the powerful mediation from early ages of the meaning attached to reading as a sociocultural activity made that activity as pervasive a phenomenon as breathing, and a phenomenon achieved under the most adverse distal conditions. The transcendent component of the mediation of reading manifested itself in a very high level of verbal fluency, a richness of vocabulary, and creativity in a variety of areas. The Rorschach protocols of Yemenite children were also shown to be rich and creative.

It is worthwhile to note that, years later. educators were shocked at the appearance of cases of illiteracy in certain Yemenite children. The lack of reading ability was clearly related to the sociocultural disintegration and disorganization of the group due to its confrontation with the dominant Israeli culture. The *mori*, a Yemenite religious teacher whose son was totally illiterate, complained to the author about his loss of authority over the boy. He pointed to the disintegration of their cultural heritage as the cause of his son's deficiency.

Juliebo (1985) discusses the cultural meaning of reading difficulties. The distal determinant, whether endogenic (genetic or organic), exogenic (environmental or educational), or emotional, is certainly responsible for certain of the individual's characteristics, but its contribution is neither direct nor unavoidable. It is only when an inadequate proximal determinant is triggered and activated that the projected problem is produced and the deleterious effects become visible. If, however, the distal determinant does not trigger the proximal determinant, by instituting an intervention program based on MLE, irrespective of whether the distal determinant was of endogenic or exogenic nature, then the outcome can be very different. Despite the presence of the triggering distal factor, if MLE is instituted, the outcome will be very different from that which is ordinarily expected.

MLE is thus perceived as a proximal factor for the evolvement of human modifiabiltiy and enables us to explain the capacity of human beings to adapt to extreme changes in their linguistic, professional, and vocational areas of functioning and need system environments. It explains, as well, the development of higher mental processes whose presence cannot be accounted for by the sole exposure to stimuli and the interaction with them.

MLE is the proximal determinant, the human ability to radically change cultural and personality styles in accordance with the demands of the new environments. Ever more astonishing is the fact that this propensity to undergo extreme changes in critical aspects of social, linguistic, and professional areas of functioning is not necessarily accompanied by a loss of self-identity, except in pathological cases.

It is this flexibility in the human psychic apparatus that is expressed in the individual's capacity to depart sharply from some characteristic critical functions, and yet to find him/herself to be identical and continuous despite the changes that have occurred. Both human modifiability and structural change include flexibility as an important component. Structural change implies the principle of transformation, which, according to Piaget, is the process by which the structure undergoes change but still preserves its nature. Flexibility can be defined as the continuity and constancy of the structure, in this case of the individual across a variety of changes that affect him/her. This contrasts strongly with what happens when a piece of iron is modified by making meaningful changes in its shape; a discontinuity in its existence is created by the produced change. This change in the iron's shape can eventually be cancelled by manipulation and the metal reshaped to its former contours. By doing so, however, the existence of the previous shape has been discontinued and a new existence started.

Changes produced in the human being, no matter how dramatic and extreme they may be, are marked by the flexibility that characterizes the person's mental condition and allows the perception, of both self and other, of an amazing sense of identity that withstands all the vicissitudes of any changes that have occurred. The continuity and constancy of the self includes the awareness and consciousness of the produced changes across stages of development—levels of functioning and competence, and ethical, civil, and occupational conditions. They are unique features of the human's mental, emotional, and personality apparatus. They have their roots in the propensity of the human being to relate to the past as a reality that is as strongly experienced, and as vividly lived, as the immediate moment. Goethe, in his introduction to *Faust*, says, "Ihr naht Euche wieder Schwankende gestalten." ("You approach me again with your shaky images.") Goethe points to the fact that these images, despite their shakiness because they belong to the past, are more vividly experienced today than when they actually happened.

Membership in a group whose culture has been transmitted to the individual by mediators considerably enlarges the existential spheres. Mediation includes the transmission of the past and this serves as the cognitive, affective, and emotional engagement toward the future. MLE, responsible for the modifiability of the human being, is thus also responsible for the flexibility that makes individuals, as well as groups, preserve their identity across their modified states. The future of both the individual and the ethnic group is strongly contingent upon the inclusion of their past into their existential sphere. Bergson (1956) has compared the relationship between the experienced past and the represented projected future to the action of shooting an arrow into the air by pulling back on the bowstring. The further back the bow is pulled, the further forward is the arrow projected. In other words, the greater the depth of the experienced past as part of the self, the further is the projection of the representational future, and the emotional orientation toward shaping this future, to continue long after one's own biological existence has come to an end. MLE thus plays a very important role in the shaping of human adaptability and of ensuring its continuity. This is done not only by enhancing individual cognitive processes, but also by creating the cognitive, emotional, and intentional conditions for the continuity of culture produced by the propensity of individuals to expand their identity—beyond their immediately experienced selves—into the past that has preceded them and the future that follows them. The emotional needs created by this past and future orientation have their origin, of course, in the biosocial nature of human existence. However, the social components have proven to be stronger than the biological factors alone, which are not able to explain the most critical characteristics of human existence.

The unique flexibility of the human cannot be explained without recourse to the mode of interaction ensured by cultural transmission on the group level and MLE on the individual level. The concept of cultural deprivation, as related to MLE, now becomes clear. Cultural deprivation due to a lack of MLE is manifested as a limited, reduced, or even total lack of modifiability in either a general or a specific area of required adaptation. Indeed, such a formulation of the very diverse phenomena of disability helps us to perceive these difficulties as structural rather than as due to some discrete distal etiology. This permits us to shape intervention processes accordingly. An attempt to remediate a particular dysfunction that is linked to a lack of modifiability requires us to increase the modifiability of the individual.

If this hypothesis, relating the origins of human intelligence defined as modifiability and flexibility to the process of MLE, is accepted, then one can derive from it the answers to two other questions posed. First, what is the role played by the cognitive phenomenon in the total of human behavior and adaptation? Second, how is the diversification in human behavior explained and what is the role that diversity plays in the continuity of human existence?

ROLE OF COGNITION IN ADAPTABILITY

The role of cognition in human adaptability has been and is still partially controversial. Modern psychology has departed from the early schools and has adopted either a dynamic or a behaviorist approach. In the dynamic approach, emotional, affective, and personality variables are considered to play the more important role in shaping the individual's behavior. The behaviorists, on the other hand, give little, if any, weight to the mental constructs that describe cognitive processes. They look only to the overt and immediately observable behavior. Only seldom do they refer to constructs such as intelligence or affectivity as engendering behavior.

During the period of the dominant impact of the psychoanalytic dynamic school, Piaget was among the first to declare cognition an important determinant of behavior. He also stressed the strong interdependence between cognition and affect by considering the two as obligatory components of each observable behavior, with cognition representing the structural aspects and affect representing the energetic factors. Cognitive-structural elements respond to questions of the what, where, when, whom, how, and how much of our actions; emotional factors respond to questions of why, what of, and what for given behavior. There is no behavior in which the two components do not converge in its production. Even in the most elementary behavior, such as instinctive behavior that is mostly determined by the inherited repertoire of inflexible, unidirectional successions of actions, certain cognitive components will be present. Sexual choices of animals are based on perceptual, sensorial, and other cognitive discriminants. We may even presume that comparative behavior determines the choice of the mate when

94

alternative choices exist.

Affectivity, representing the energetic factor, both generates and is generated by cognitive processes. Thus, motivation and attitudes cannot be considered in isolation from such cognitive factors as knowledge, operations, anticipation of outcomes, and adoption of strategies for achieving particular goals. The choice of one's goals and aims is strongly contingent upon cognitive functions and mental acts by which one singles them out of a number of possible alternatives, using comparison in order to ascribe priorities to one as opposed to another. This view of cognition as generating affective, emotional, and motivational elements may be contrasted with the view of dynamic depth psychology that conceives of the development of cognitive processes as secondary to the affective, emotional primary core. In the very succinct representation of affectivity in his work, Piaget describes affectivity as closely following the changes in the individual's cognitive structure along the developmental stages and the successive appearance of formal mental operations.

We prefer to view the relationship between the two as the two sides of a transparent coin, with the shape being meaningfully affected by the changes that are undergone on each side of the coin. Today, the cognitive determinants of our behavior are considered more important than ever. The need to adapt, i.e., to change, one's behavior, in order to make it correspond to changes in the situation with which one is confronted, is nowadays so strong that we may consider "modifiability," defining the concept of intelligence, as the most vital condition for survival. Cognitive modifiability, in this sense, should be considered the prime goal not only of education in the initial stages of the human organism, but it must also be implanted where it is missing or increased when the need to change and become modified is exacerbated by the individual's existential condition.

A student, exhausted in preparing himself for an entrance

exam, said, "Now that I no longer have this goal, I have nothing to do. I wish I could go to sleep until I have a new goal to put me to work again." The difficulty in adapting himself to the new situation of aimlessness orients this individual to escape into sleep. The same is true for millions of people who retire at relatively early ages and find it extremely difficult to adapt to the new role retirement imposes on them. Changes in role, in techniques, and in instrumentation all require an openness, a propensity to learn and become modified by it. It is this openness to learn and become meaningfully modified in formally organized, as well as situationally determined, encounters that is missing in many individuals and may be considered a lack of intelligence or a lack of capacity. Indeed, modifiability is lacking due to a variety of endogenous or exogenous factors that have triggered a reduced MLE; however, these should be considered states of the organism and its cognitive structure rather than immutable, hard-wired traits. The former are modifiable; the latter, fixed and immutable. Scheffler (1985) points to the modifiability of the potential in all three dimensions of this construct.

FACTORS DETERMINING DIVERSITY OF MODIFIABILITY

What are the factors that determine the diversity of human modifiability, both in terms of level of functioning and in variations in the nature of the functioning, differences in cognitive styles, and personality? The issue of the level of functioning has been discussed at some length as the outcome of an individual's level of modifiability. The benefits derived by the individual from mediated experiences manifest themselves in adaptive behavior. The view of intelligence as a dynamic process-oriented concept whose major characteristics are the modifiability and the constant changes that the structure of the mind undergoes has two implications: flexibility and diversification. The MLE hypothesis, as it is operationalized in its twelve parameters, considers these two factors as the differential outcome of the various parameters. The first three: mediation of intentionality and reciprocity, mediation of transcendence, and mediation of meaning are the universal criteria of MLE. An interaction that is not shaped by these three parameters cannot claim the quality of the interaction we attribute to MLE.

Intentionality turns the stimuli impinging on the organism from a random probabilistic appearance into an organized, directional succession, with characteristics lent to it by the mediator's culturally determined intentions. The mediator's intention modifies the stimulus in order to ensure its registration by the mediatee. Thus the *intensity*, the *frequency*, and the *modality* of its appearance are regulated by the mediator's intention. The effects of this intention are not limited to the stimulus or even to being registered. The intention changes the mediatee's state of mind, level of vigilance and alertness, and even what Herbartian pedagogy refers to as the "learner's apperceptive state" (which can be equated with the process of sensitization to certain stimuli by relating them to a schemata established by the mediator). This change in the mediatee's mental state, provoked by the mediator, turns the interaction into a source of structural schemata whose active components will affect the individual's mode of dealing with a variety of stimuli. The mediator's intention, which animates her/his interactive behavior, also changes her/him in some critical aspects (see Beck [1965] for Herbart).

The second parameter that has a universal role is the mediation of transcendence. The mediator does not limit the length and breadth of the interaction to those parts of the situation that have originally initiated the interaction. Rather he/she widens the scope of the interaction to areas that are consonant with more remote goals. By way of illustration, if the child points to an orange and asks what it is, a nonmediated answer will be limited to the simple labeling of the object in question. A mediated transcendent interaction will offer a categorical classifying definition: "It's the fruit of a plant, a tree. There are many fruits similar to the orange: a lemon, a mandarin, etc. They are all juicy. Some are sweet, some sour; some are big, others small. They are all citrus." In transcending the immediacy of the required interaction, the mediator establishes a way in which the mediatee can relate objects and events to broader systems, categories, and classes. Creating the search for similarities and differences, systems of operations are established that will act as a way by which the individual can register the information reaching him/her by direct exposure to the stimuli. The transcending principle of MLE is not only responsible for the widening of the cognitive factors, but also for the constant enlargement of the need systems that act as energetic determinants of continuous change and development via intrinsic motivation.

Transcendence is seldom, if at all, observed among animals. Thus, the cat, teaching her kittens to do their little job in the garden, is evidently animated by an intention. It is reflected in the mother cat's waiting until all the kittens can see her act as model. But this animal's intention is limited to a particular and discrete behavior with very little, if any, spillover to other activities. Of necessity, it rests within the limits of the organism's primary instinctual needs. The transcendent nature of MLE is the most humanizing of the parameters that reflect the quality of the MLE interaction.

The third parameter universally necessary in all MLE interactions is the mediation of meaning. This parameter reflects the need systems of the mediators as a determinant of their intention and their perception of the goals for the future that they set for themselves and their progeny or their mediatees. The mediation of meaning provides the energetic, dynamic source of power that will ensure that the mediational interaction will be experienced by the mediatee. On a more general level, the mediation of meaning becomes the generator of the emotional, motivational, attitudinal, and value-oriented behaviors of the individual.

Intentionality and transcendence present the mediatee with the structure of mental behavior. To a large extent they provide answers to the questions of what to see, where to look, how much to invest in perceiving a particular stimulus or event, how to organize the succession of events so as to lead to a particular goal, how to integrate all the parts of the event into the whole that will permit the solution of the problem at hand. The mediated meaning will generate the answers to the why and what for of these mental or motor acts.

To summarize, the first three parameters are responsible for what we consider the unique features of human existence, its modifiability and flexibility. They are the most stable and universal qualities, and as such are common to all human existence, irrespective of cultural, socioeconomic, or educational levels of functioning. Modifiability is accessible to all individuals or groups whose level of functioning is extremely damaged because of their cultural difference, cultural deprivation (lack of MLE), or impairments due to endogenous or exogenous factors. Modifiability is considered possible even at advanced ages. The mediation of intentionality, transcendence, and meaning may have to be varied in terms of intensity, frequency, content, and language in order to overcome the particular barriers and resistances created by the condition, age, and particular characteristics of the individual. However, the hypothesis of MLE as the proximal determinant of differential cognitive development points to the ways of increasing individuals' modifiability, irrespective of their condition.

The diversification of cultural cognitive styles and emotional behavior can be ascribed to the eight or more parameters that have been described elsewhere. They include the mediation of a feeling of competence; mediation of regulation and control of behavior; mediation of sharing behavior; mediation of individuation and psychological differentiation; mediation of goal-seeking, goal-setting, planning, and goal-achieving behavior; mediation for challenge: the search for novelty and complexity; mediation of the awareness of change; and mediation of an optimistic approach. These parameters are not to be considered exhaustive but rather as a first selection of qualities of interaction that may, but need not, appear in each interaction in order to turn it into an MLE. The presence of any of these parameters is situationally determined and varies greatly according to societal, environmental, and cultural factors.

The mediation of psychological differentiation is not possible in each mediator-mediatee interaction. A teacher who is interested in a solidification of a learned activity through its repetition cannot encourage learners to act differently from the models they are supposed to repeat or to express their differentiated personalities. Thus, mediation of psychological differentiation and individuation is not a necessary quality of MLE. Furthermore, there are cultures that do not consider individuation as a desirable objective for their members and do little to encourage the process. An enlarged family in a tribal setting, for example, does not give first priority to the process of individuation.

Ecological, historical, and cultural factors will all determine the extent to which the various parameters of MLE will be mediated, transmitted, and reinforced. It is this differential mediation that determines the diversification that is characteristic of the human. Although the animal realm also undergoes processes of diversification, it is totally contingent on the changes in the ecosystem of the animal; the human is much less dependent on the ecosystem. Cultural transmission plays a much more important role in determining the nature of an individual's cognitive style, personality, emotional responses to constraints, or even to the options presented by the physical environment. The human being's alloplastic defense has changed many of the environmental conditions to make them suitable to his/her needs and states of mind. Thus, for example, when the process of individuation became a cultural imposition, segregation from the enlarged family made it necessary to overcome the issue of distances by the proliferation of individual cars.

Another MLE parameter that varies greatly from situation to situation, from person to person, and even more, from culture to culture, is the mediated regulation of behavior. This parameter deals with the individual's orientation toward the use of cognitive as well as metacognitive means to initiate or delay responses: to control and inhibit behavior, and to accelerate certain responses according to criteria established through cognition. The regulation of behavior is extremely important in occidental culture where the technologically advanced society requires a highly controlled and regulated mode of behavior. This can be contrasted with the lesser demands for regulation and control in the more natural and rustic life that encourages spontaneous uninhibited, often impulsive behaviors.

In describing the various cognitive styles, Sternberg considers them to be largely the outcome of social, cultural, and environmental factors. Thus, judicial, legislative, and executive styles, which describe variations among individuals in the preferential modes of the use of their intelligence, are not only considered the outcome of inherited trends, but to a much larger extent, the result of culture, gender, age, parenting style, and schooling. To consider these variations as socialized ipso facto is to view them as modifiable at least to some degree; indeed, one of Sternberg's hopes is to be able to teach students to use various styles "flexibly" as an optimal mode of adaptation (Sternberg, Chapter 2 of this book).

DIVERSIFICATION AS MLE GOAL

As mentioned previously, the second outcome of MLE, after the promotion of flexibility and modifiability, is diversification. The diversification of human states, orientations, motivations, and those described by the eight parameters of MLE represent modes of adaptation of the individual to his/her sociocultural environment. The modes give the individual the feeling of identity as part of the group to which he/she belongs.

Modifiability, flexibility, differentiation, and diversification cannot be explained solely by direct and unmediated exposure to stimuli, no matter how rich nor how diverse the stimuli, and no matter how actively the individual interacts with them. In order to benefit from such exposures, one must be sensitized by the process of mediation. Those who have not been exposed to MLE, for various possible reasons, may not benefit meaningfully from their exposure to stimuli. In Piagetian terminology, their schemata are not flexible enough to permit them to be affected by the assimilation of new stimuli. Thus, the process of accommodation does not automatically follow; the individual is then not modified by an encounter with these stimuli. The same is true for the diversification and differentiation of the individual. The development of differential cognitive and personality styles is strongly dependent on the prior mediational experience of the individual.

ETHNIC GROUP ANALYSIS

The effects of MLE on the modifiability and flexibility of the individual are best illustrated by relating the level of modifiability of certain ethnic groups to the mediational and transmissional processes typical of the particular culture.

Our encounter with the Yemenite children who arrived in Israel in the Magic Carpet operation of 1945–1948 first made us aware that a very low level of functioning could coexist in individuals with a very rich culture that differentiated between these individuals and other groups and provided them with a well-defined identity. One of the characteristics of such a group is its high level of modifiability. Indeed, the Yemenites proved they were able to learn and modify their functioning meaningfully. On the other hand, during the long years of our work in Youth Aliyah, we were confronted with children from other ethnic groups who had great difficulty in changing their levels of functioning. The differences between these two types of ethnic groups were not in their manifest levels of functioning (which were equally low), but rather in their levels of modifiability. The ease and pervasiveness of change that one group displayed contrasted sharply with the difficulties of the other group in adapting to the new culture and its requirements.

In an attempt to explain the striking difference in modifiability between groups who were otherwise similar in their low manifest cognitive, academic, technological, and occupational level of functioning, we looked into the cultural antecedents of the two groups. This allowed us first to hypothesize that the level of modifiability is directly related to the differential level of cultural transmission in each of these cultures. Only after many years of study have we been able to conclude that a sharp distinction must be made between cultural difference and cultural deprivation as the source of difficulties in the adaptation of the individual to a new culture.

When immigrating into a new and different dominant culture, the culturally different individual may prove to be a fast learner of those parameters of functioning that are the most critical for adaptation to the dominant society. Despite the fact that they are culturally different and devoid of certain linguistic, conceptual, and technological skills, there are immigrants from developing countries who show an amazing propensity to modify their level of functioning by using their areas of strength and adapting them to the requirements of the strange and often hostile dominant culture. In many cases, this propensity to learn and become modified through this learning makes them achieve high levels of functioning and efficiency despite their low level of language mastery and limited orientation in other crucial areas. Thus, cultural difference not only does not hamper adaptation, as was previously assumed by sociologists referring to the culturally different as the traditional society, but such difference may actually prove to be an enhancing factor of adaptation.

Cultural difference must be contrasted with the phenomenon of cultural deprivation. In this context, cultural deprivation is defined as the alienation of groups, or of individuals, from their own culture. An individual who has not been exposed to MLE or could not benefit from it is marked by low modifiability and a limited propensity to benefit from direct exposure to stimuli and events. Even when culturally deprived persons are better equipped linguistically and with other skills required by the new dominant culture, their adaptation is far inferior to that of the culturally different. Often, the culturally deprived are born within the dominant culture, living side by side with the socializing and educational agents of this majority culture. Yet they are totally unaffected either by this proximity or by the attempts to orient them to adaptation.

A good illustration is the story of R whose parents were highly cultured people involved in the arts. Their excellent financial status enabled them to travel and to provide a very rich and highly stimulating environment for their children. None of their children, however, was able to benefit from this rich world of informal learning opportunities. Furthermore, they were even less prepared to make use of their school experiences. One of them, R, was declared mentally defective—a diagnosis that was disproved by our dynamic assessment. Other children of the family were considered learning disabled, differing among themselves only in the degree of severity.

The author was able to trace this condition to a family constellation that obstructed the parent-child mediational interaction to the extent that it left the children alone in the exciting world in which they lived. They were unable to utilize their family experiences beyond the immediate gratification they were provided. Thus, at the age of fifteen, when R was asked to say something about the many countries he had visited, not only was he unable to name the countries, but he could not even remember, except for some rudimentary recollection, where he had been or with whom. This was his condition despite a good memory as revealed by dynamic testing. Further, R could not distinguish one place from another and could not relate places to times of visit. It became clear, and the parents confirmed, that these cognitive parameters were never discussed with the children before, during, or after the visits. This was also true for many other experiences that left no traces in R's repertoire. At the age of fifteen, for example, R could not relate ice, water, and steam as the three conditions of matter (solid, liquid, and gas), and considered them as isolated, disparate substances. The author was so surprised by R's ignorance that he reacted insensitively, regretfully hurting the boy's feelings. This incident clearly shows how little we adults, teachers, and parents are aware of the gaps, not only in knowledge, but, even more, in the prerequisites of learning that are necessary to turn experiences into effective tools for further learning.

Years later, when interviewed by a journalist, R recalled this episode: "I had seen ice turning into water, and water into steam, and yet couldn't see them as products of the transformation process of one and the same matter." R unwittingly described the characteristic shared by many of the culturally deprived. That is, an episodic grasp of reality makes the individual passively experience the perceived stimuli without relating them to either what has preceded and, even less, to what is expected to follow. An episodic grasp of reality makes learning from experience, with its subsequent changes in the individual's cognitive structure, almost impossible. Individuals or groups that have been offered MLE or received cultural transmission have been equipped with effective modes of perceiving and elaborating their perceptions. This permits them to learn to generalize by actively linking their various life experiences through comparing, coding, and decoding them, by summing up the times of their occurrence, by relating them to the time and space of their occurrence, etc. Out of this linking process, concepts, categories, classes, series, codes, symbols, causal relationships, teleological relationships, and other hierachically higher levels of functioning are derived. Their origins cannot be traced back to the sole and direct interaction between the organism and sources of stimuli. Rather, all these modes of mental acts have their origin in socially determined, human-based mediational interactions. In the recently published posthumous writings of Vygotsky (Minick 1986; Wertsch 1984), the social process is seen as crucial to the development of human mental activities.

No matter how extreme the difference between culturally different individuals and the cultural environment in which they live, they will be able to learn the new culture and adapt to it by capitalizing on the attitudes, dispositions, modes of focusing and search they have acquired through MLE. In their study of cognitive profiles of different ethnic groups, Lesser, Fifer, and Clark (1965) bring indirect evidence of the difference between the culturally different and the culturally deprived. Members of the culturally different group have profiles that commonly identify a high percentage of the group's population. This relatively strong identity is also marked by a higher level of cognitive functioning. In contrast, the culturally deprived group has a very limited number of people with identical profiles. By the same token, they have a very low level of functioning. The Yemenites, for example, who have developed a very strong identity as a culturally different group, have proven to have had a tremendous influence on Israeli cultural development. Their contributions to music, dance, fashion, and culinary arts have been eagerly accepted by the more advanced and more veteran members of the dominant culture. This Israeli example proves that the dominant culture has accommodated itself to the Yemenites by its assimilation of these cultural values. The integration of culturally different individuals is, of course, strongly contingent upon opportunities they are offered to respond to the strong need to adapt and the pull exerted on them by an advantaged model of the culturally dominant group.

Opportunities for educational and occupational mobility are necessary for cultural accommodation. Whenever they exist, the culturally different group will take advantage of them. This is not always the case with culturally deprived individuals. Devoid of the prerequisites of learning, due to the lack of MLE and cultural transmission, the culturally deprived person often is unable to identify the new goals that life in the more advantaged and higher functioning environment offers. Furthermore, the culturally deprived person is not inclined to identify with these goals. A host of cognitive deficiencies are responsible for this person's limited capacity to benefit from the opportunities to learn, to change, to increase the repertoire of adaptive behaviors and to apply them to situations, such as those produced by immigration, or by radical changes in occupational, social, and even moral lifestyles. Such cognitive deficiencies include the lack of future, anticipatory, planning behavior; the lack of need for logical evidence; a limited capacity to define problems and inner and outer sources of disequilibrium; the lack of comparative behavior that would permit the distinction between the familiar and unfamiliar, the known and the unknown, and the advantages and disadvantages of certain behaviors; the lack of a capacity to create systems of priorities consonant with more meaningful needs; the lack of use of several sources of information; the inadequate control over one's behavior, making impulsivity the most modal behavior of the individual; a limited representation leading to reliance on the immediately perceived, and the lack of orientation toward using the past and future as sources of guidance for present behavior; a cognitively determined egocentricity; and other deficiencies (see Figure 2, List of Deficient Cognitive Functions).

As long as culturally deprived individuals continue to live in a familiar environment that they have mastered by over-learning (and by being born into), they may not show signs of disadaptation. The real problem for the culturally deprived starts when the environment requires more than very limited adaptation, when they cannot survive without change. It is then that the deficient functions, resulting from a lack of MLE, have their negative impact and create conflicts whose solutions may

107

Figure 2
List of Deficient Cognitive Functions

Impairments Affecting the Input, Elaborational, and Output Levels of Cognitive Functioning

Input Level

1. Blurred and sweeping perception
2. Unplanned, impulsive, and unsystematic exploratory behavior
3. Lack of impaired, receptive verbal tools that affect discrimination (e.g., objects, events, relationships, etc., do not have appropriate labels)
4. Lack of, or impaired, spatial orientation; the lack of stable systems of reference impairs the establishment of topological and Euclidean organization of space
5. Lack of, or impaired, temporal concepts
6. Lack of, or impaired, conservation of constancies (size, shape, quantity, orientation) across variation in these factors
7. Lack of, or deficient need for, precision and accuracy in data gathering
8. Lack of capacity for considering two or more sources of information at once; this is reflected in dealing with data in a piecemeal fashion rather than as a unit of organized facts

Elaborational Level

1. Inadequacy in the perception of the existence and definition of an actual problem
2. Inability to select relevant vs. nonrelevant cues in defining a problem
3. Lack of spontaneous comparative behavior or limitation of its application by a restricted need system
4. Narrowness of the mental field
5. Episodic grasp of reality
6. Lack of, or impaired, need for pursuing logical evidence
7. Lack of, or impaired, interiorization
8. Lack of, or impaired, inferential-hypothetical, 'iffy' thinking
9. Lack of, or impaired, strategies for hypothesis testing
10. Lack of, or impaired, ability to define the framework necessary for problem-solving behavior
11. Lack of, or impaired, planning behavior
12. Nonelaboration of certain cognitive categories because the verbal

concepts are not a part of the individual's verbal inventory (on a receptive level) or they are not mobilized at the expressive level

Output Level

1. Egocentric communicational modalities
2. Difficulties in projecting virtual relationships
3. Blocking
4. Trial-and-error responses
5. Lack of, or impaired, verbal tools for communicating adequately elaborated responses
6. Lack of, or impaired, need for precision and accuracy in communicating one's response
7. Deficiency of visual transport
8. Impulsive, acting-out behavior

not be adequate. Drastic changes in environment through migration or the need to shift from an overlearned, routine, mechanically mastered activity may bring with them states of extreme disadaptation because of the incapacity of individuals, devoid of the prerequisites of learning, to acquire the necessary new skills for their adaptation.

These situations are well known for both children and adults in recent historic occurrences of large-scale migration. In many countries with high technological and educational levels, new immigrants appear unable to cope, and therefore react in ways that have become detrimental both to themselves and to the absorbing society. The author was confronted with the problems of such an ethnic group that came to Israel. (For obvious reasons, the author will disclose neither the name of the group nor its country of origin.) When placed in instructional, educational, and social situations shaped by the dominant culture, the difficulties manifested by the group were so great that strong negative stereotypes emerged regarding the normalcy of the members of this group in terms of their IQ, intelligence, and the integrity of their central nervous systems. In the prognosis for their adaptation and the possible effects of education, some members of the dominant society asked: "Are these people educable?"

A group of psychologists examined 300 children belonging to this group with the Bender-Gestalt test. On the basis of the very low test results, the professionals seriously considered the possibility of minimal brain damage or a certain degree of immaturity of the central nervous system in the children. The author was able to reject this notion by pointing out that an investment in the nature of a mediational interaction on the part of the examiner succeeded to a large degree in wiping out the traces of the hypothesized "minimal brain damage" in many of the cases discussed. Nevertheless, the difficulties manifested by the group were pervasive and affected the children's personalities and emotional states. Extreme levels of anxiety were observed on a behavioral level, as well as subclinically as indicated by Rorschach and other types of observations. A deeper analysis of the deficiencies revealed the cognitive origin of this anxiety that rendered these individuals totally helpless in the confrontation with the new reality. The children could not perceive the character of this new environment, or see what in it was common or different from what was already known. They were rendered unable to anticipate or predict the outcome of their behavior and were, therefore, in a state of cognitive "blindness." Many of the inadaptive reactions that characterized the members of this particular group were attributable to their state of cultural deprivation.

This ethnic group became alienated from its own cultural patrimony. Historical reasons were responsible for the social disorganization and the disruption of traditional social processes. Societal agents, who had previously been charged with fulfilling the role of social and cultural mediators were no longer effective. Internal migration, the loss of the extended family's support, and the limited capacity of the nuclear family to supply mediational needs, interrupted the processes of mediation and cultural transmission necessary for cognitive and emotional development of the children.

It took time and a meaningful investment from both the planners of integration and the leaders emerging from the group itself to reorient the group toward its past, its cultural mores and values. After this occurred, a very meaningful change became apparent in individual members of the group. Today in Israel, this group has become one of the most active agents in leading a revival and revitalization process of its own ethnic culture. Pride in their ethnicity has positively affected the ability of individuals to integrate into the dominant culture as members of their own culture. The current impact of this group on Israeli society surpasses even that of the Yemenites.

In this context, another example worthy of mention is the Native American, particularly the Navajo, with whom the author and many of his colleagues have had the opportunity of working. The preservation and enrichment of their culture and language are seen by native peoples as hinges upon which their survival and integrity exist. On the other hand, there are the policymakers and theoreticians who believe there is a diametric opposition between the American and Indian cultures. They hold that the "Indian ways," cultural values, tribal history, and language must be sacrificed to usher the Native American properly into contemporary American society.

In effect, the denial of value, the loss of orientation toward the nation's past, the rejection of its language and symbols constituted a real depletion of the internal identity and readiness of the Indian youth to identify. The degree of cultural deprivation observed on the reservation was certainly extreme. Some of the group's leaders, becoming aware of the role of MLE in the development of cognitive processes, perceived the extremely negative results of the lack of MLE in the cognitive, social, and emotional condition of the Navajo reservation's youth, in their low level of performance, in their trend to drop out of school, and in their lack of need for adaptation manifested in the proliferation of alcoholism, drug abuse, and juvenile suicide (known to be very high among these young people). A few of the Navajo nation's leaders have adopted the philosophy and theory of Structural Cognitive Modifiability in general, and MLE in particular, as a way to enhance the cognitive and affective condition of their children and, by the same token, they use the theory of MLE as the rationale for reviving the cultural patrimony of the Navajo nation (Emerson 1986).

MLE has been deemed the most effective theory and applied system to reorient both Navajo juveniles and adults, to offer a legitimization to reinstituting the native language ("dena") as the language of instruction, to turn to history as a source of identity and, as some of them put it very clearly, "to become better Americans by being good Indians." Members of the Native American community face a variety of general problems that they hope to approach through an application of the theory of MLE. First is their desire for the community control of education with the right to reinstitute the Indian language in schools. Self-determination in schools involves decision-making authority over academics, instruction, student guidance and activities, parental involvement, and fiscal and administrative matters. General community development, as well as tribal economic development, will also be affected by MLE programs that, among other things, teach management, analyses, decision among alternatives, projection of relationships, goal setting, planning, and goal achieving. Emerson summarizes the Native American belief that culture and cognition are linked: "By singing our own songs, we can increase our chances for better and more comfortable lives for our youth and ourselves in the present and future society" (Emerson 1985, p. 15).

Some of the systems derived from MLE and its philosophy—the Learning Potential Assessment Device (LPAD) and the Instrumental Enrichment (IE) programs—have been applied in the Navajo community (Emerson 1986). Reports on the effects of the implementation of dynamic assessment, intervention for cognitive development, and MLE, though scarce, are highly encouraging. The interest in the adaptation of the theory and practices of MLE has been extended to other Native American groups in the United States and the Northern Canadian Territories. A number of these tribes are using the theory of MLE as a basis for lobbying for the right to institute their languages in their respective schools and to control these schools and the general education of their children themselves as a way to ensure cultural transmission.

Another group that has shown the impact of MLE in the most extreme way are the Jewish Ethiopians of color who immigrated from Africa to Israel in the mid-1980s. The "Falashim," as they were once called (they prefer to be called Ethiopians because of the pejorative meaning of Falashim, Hebrew for "intruders"), represent the greatest distance from the dominant Israeli culture in many areas. Until recently, only a very limited number of these Ethiopians, also called Beta-Israel in our studies, were literate. They had neither prayer books nor books of commentary for Bible study. The group's level of technology was extremely rudimentary, with shepherding and elementary agriculture as the main occupations. Their housing, simple clay huts, was primitive, as was their use of utensils. Despite certain significant differences among them, this was true for the majority of the Ethiopian Jewish population.

The fact that the Ethiopian group's entire identity and affiliation to Judaism was based on their origins dating back 2500 years created an almost unbridgeable gap between them and the current dominant Israeli culture. Yet, they were all but culturally deprived. They were culturally different from the Israeli culture, as well as from the surrounding Ethiopian culture, by virtue of very rich articulation of rites, mores, and styles that had been acquired through an elaborate process of mediation and cultural transmission. Illiteracy had made it totally impossible for this cultural transmission to go through impersonal channels, such as reading, writing, radio, or television. All cultural transmission had to be oral-aural, from mouth to ear. This situation probably has had a highly beneficial effect, however. The Ethiopian priest ("the kess"), the religious head of the community, would speak in front of a gathering for hours under the worst climactic conditions. Those among us who have seen children and adults listening, focusing on a speaker for hours without moving, without any sign of impatience, are aware of the effects of such an exposure on the attentional processes of individuals. Those who study the observable behaviors of Ethiopian children and adolescents are amazed by the richness and particularities of their style, which could not have been developed without intensive mediation, through observation, and by verbal and nonverbal MLE involving intentionality, transcendence, and meaning.

The power of the early mediational interactions in this African ethnic group is evidenced by the variety of styles and behaviors that are characteristic of the total Ethiopian Jewish community. These differ greatly from both the culture with which they were previously surrounded in Ethiopia, and even more so from the groups of cultural difference in Israel. The results of extensive testing of the Ethiopian children with the LPAD in its group form provide us with fascinating preliminary information on Beta-Israel (see Kaniel, Tzuriel, Feuerstein, Ben Shachar, and Eitan 1986).

The group LPAD (consisting of the following tasks: Raven Progressive Matrices; LPAD Variations I and II; Organization of Dots; Complex Figure; Organizer; Numerical Progressions and Figural Progressions) was administered to the 316 adolescents, average age of 15.7. In the experimental group, 75 percent of the population were girls; 25 percent, boys. Each of the tasks, except for the Raven Progressive Matrices, was administered in three stages: premediation, mediation, and post-mediation. The Raven was administered pre- and post-without mediation. Ethiopian adolescents of similar demographic characteristics served as a control group and received the same tasks with essentially the same procedure, but with no mediation between exposures.

Results obtained on these Ethiopians were compared between the experimental and control groups, as well as with data gathered from studies with the same tasks with culturally deprived and regular Israeli adolescents. Results revealed that in all tasks, the experimental group benefited from the mediation given them in terms of learning and transfer as compared to the control group (see Table 1). The performance level of the experimental group was similar to that of regular Israeli groups that had been dynamically assessed (see Table 2). Finally, results indicate that mediation changed the curve of distribution for all participants. Since most of the subjects performed very well in the post-mediation phase, it seemed impossible to predict post-mediation performance from premediation scores (see Table 3). The correlation between the pre- and the post-test was

115

Table 1

Averages in Percentages and Standard Deviations
(in parentheses) for Each of the Tasks
on Raven's Progressive Matrices
in the Control and Experimental Groups

	Experimental group	Control group	t text
Raven pre-	36.45 (19.40)	39.39 (15.46)	
Raven post	59.46 (20.13)	42.50 (19.62)	* *
Variation I	68.59 (26.77)	27.44 (15.84)	* * *
Variation II	64.57 (21.18)	20.69 (10.23)	* * *
Numerical Progression before intervention	46.22 (22.43)	36.00 (17.48)	
Numerical Progression after intervention	62.02 (22.74)	29.87 (18.21)	* * *
Figural Progression before intervention	61.80 (25.74)	57.57 (26.39)	
Figural Progression after intervention	80.70 (20.48)	60.42 (24.49)	* *
Organizer before intervention	34.99 (25.09)	26.86 (13.23)	
Organizer after intervention	68.74 (27.75)	30.26 (19.49)	* * *
Organization of Dots	86.74 (22.41)	59.49 (35.93)	* *
Complex Figure before intervention	55.14 (25.05)	61.42 (22.71)	
Complex Figure after intervention	88.14 (14.57)	64.28 (26.42)	* *

***P<0.001   **P<0.01

Table 2
Averages in Percentages and Standard Deviations (in parentheses) on the various Raven Matrices in the Experimental and Control Groups

	Experimental group		Control group	
	First time	Second time	First time	Second time
Raven (all 60 items	36.45 (19.40)	59.46 (20.13)	39.39 (15.46)	42.50 (19.62)
B8–B12 in the Raven	25.96 (33.47)	65.61 (34.67)	32.65 (33.09)	45.50 (35.37)
5 items C-D-E in the Raven	15.17 (17.74)	39.16 (26.15)	16.33 (17.16)	20.50 (16.00)
Modifiability in Raven 50 items with no intervention	39.62 (19.82)	60.88 (19.52)	42.37 (16.02)	44.40 (19.64)

Table 3
Raw Scores (total – 60) and Percentiles
in the Raven for various groups

	Raven pre-	Percentile	Raven post	Percentile
Ethiopians age 16	22	less than 5	36	25
Culturally Deprived age 14	39	35	44	50
Israeli Adolescents age 14	37	25	42	40
Standard Norms age 13–25	44	50		no data

Data on Raven percentiles and norms from J. E. Orme (1966), *Human Development.*

low. The high level of modifiability evident in the results of the assessment left little doubt that the Ethiopian population was culturally different and not culturally deprived.

Indeed, the readiness and propensity to learn revealed by the Ethiopians' performance has become renowned in Israel; it is described by all persons who have worked with them. Educators claim they have seldom seen a group that has acquired literacy so rapidly despite its previous little, if any, exposure to symbols and signs. Despite the fact that the Ethiopian Jews immigrated after decades of oppression, and underwent harrowing trials and unbelievable suffering on their way to Israel—which some have equated with the experience of the Holocaust—they have shown considerable resilience and readiness in order to adapt to the requirements of the open Israeli society with its constantly changing technology. Their adaptation has not been a matter of merely narrowing a gap, but of making a major, difficult transition from a rural, traditional, closed society whose theme was survival, preservation of the status quo, and transmission of culture intact from one generation to the next. (See Figures 3 and 4.)

The Ethiopians' social mobility, based mainly upon the acquisition of the repertoire of basic school skills, of information necessary for solving their problems, of modalities of functioning that respond to the requirements of the society in which they live, has made many of these extremely different children accede to levels of functioning that would have been totally inaccessible to them without the deep changes they underwent. However, the modifiability they displayed in learning to read and write, in acquiring the basic school skills and the operations of mathematics became a source of disappointment once difficulties were revealed in their adapting to higher mental processes, such as abstract thinking. What went wrong in the Ethiopian children's development?

Figure 3
Comparison Between Beta-Israel and Israeli Adolescents
on Raven Progressive Matrices Test (pre- and post-scores)

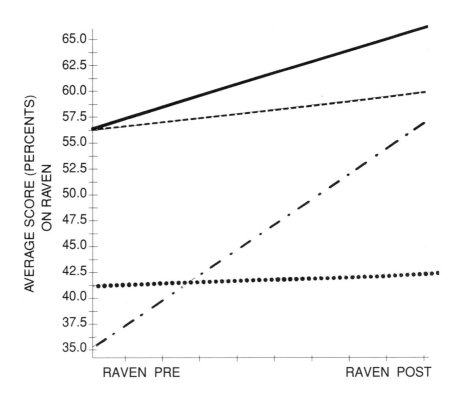

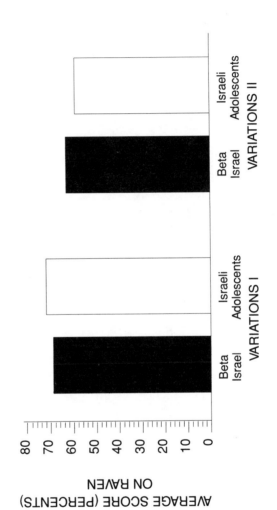

Figure 4
Comparison Between Beta-Israel and
Israeli Adolescents on Variations Tasks

121

Teachers, educators, and caregivers had wrongly assumed that the same rapidity and efficiency the Ethiopians had shown in the acquisition of basic school skills would continue with the same rhythm and ease in areas of conceptualized abstract thinking without requiring further intervention. This erroneous assumption did not consider the need of the culturally different to receive mediation in areas that are not constructed by the process of unfolding or maturation, but rather are the product of specific mediation without which they could not be acquired. The genetic view of development and the idea that formal operations develop as a natural result of the combined effects of maturation and active interaction with stimuli and experience have adversely affected educators. It was considered totally unnecessary and superfluous to mediate to individuals the need for logical thinking, the need for comparative behavior, the use of multiple sources of information, representation, and the need for inferential thinking.

In the case of the Ethiopians, it was falsely expected that once they mastered basic school skills, they would be able to accede (without any additional intervention in hierarchically higher cognitive functions and operations) to the types of thinking necessary for higher academic studies. To the great distress of all involved, however, from a group of twenty Ethiopians who had been given a year's preparatory studies for university entrance, only one student was able to pass the entrance examination. The preparatory studies consisted of content knowledge. The failure of the university candidates made some of the policymakers involved in the education planning question their previous assumptions about the group members' intelligence and their potential for higher education.

The University Student Counseling Services, alerted to the problem, took upon itself a project of promoting cognitive abilities and facilitating the absorption processes of the Ethiopian students. Each student received the IE program twice a week, with additional enrichment specific to the demands of the university. As a result, of the fifteen students who finished the new preparatory program, nine were accepted to regular university studies. It was necessary for the others to receive additional intervention before they could be accepted. As the director of the Student Counseling Services stated, "We believe that one of the major factors in the matrix of their studies which resulted in the increase in the students' level of achievement was Instrumental Enrichment" (Kron 1986).

The culturally different, even though modifiable, need to become equipped with conceptual, relational, operational, and linguistic tools that are not currently in their repertoire in order to succeed in their adaptation to the dominant culture. Once such a systematic investment is made, however, structured cognitive modifiability, which is the result of early MLE, permits the individual to benefit rapidly.

SUMMARY AND CONCLUSION

In conclusion, we would like to review what we previously presented in this chapter and briefly discuss some of its implications.

First, we attempted to outline the elements with which a theory of intelligence should deal, and to describe some of the components with a certain amount of detail. In defining intelligence, we proposed to relate to intelligence as to a dynamic process rather than as to a reified entity and a set of disparate more or less defined factors. In this sense, intelligence becomes the process of adaptability itself. It includes a large variety of modalities of adaptation, whose orientation may be either positive or negative, depending upon the context and differential goals of the adaptation.

We then discussed at some length the origins of human modifiability as compared to the adaptability of other existences (e.g., animal) and described the concept of Mediated Learning Experiences (MLE) as fulfilling two different roles. The first is explicative; the second, heuristic. MLE is thus the pivotal element of our theory and forms the basis for the applied systems derived from the theory of Structural Cognitive Modifiability: the Learning Potential Assessment Device (LPAD), Instrumental Enrichment (IE), and the shaping of modifying environments. These three applied systems represent a succession of steps derived from the belief that the human being is indeed modifiable and that MLE plays a key role in the evolvement of the human being's flexibility and plasticity.

The LPAD basically relates to the question of modifiability and its evaluation. Our reasoning suggests that, if indeed modifiability does exist and is accessible to a great number of individuals, then one must be able to evaluate it. We do not seek to measure it. The LPAD is based on a test-mediation-test model. In the first stage, a baseline is established. In the second stage, intervention is focused and aims at producing specific or general changes. In the course of all three phases, the process of change, rather than its product, is evaluated and used to answer a number of questions concerning the particular individual:

- Is the individual as modifiable as the general postulate claims?
- Are differential levels of modifiabiltiy contingent on the individual's condition, the baseline, and a variety of other determinants, such as the amount of MLE to which the individual was exposed?
- What is the nature and extent of changes one can hope for?
- What is the nature and quantity of mediation necessary to produce long-term and permanent desired changes?

The LPAD is oriented toward establishing a profile of modifiability and determining the preferential modality by which this modifiability can be materialized. Indeed, it has proven to be a very useful tool in the attempt to change not only individuals, but systems as well.

As its major goal, the IE program seeks to increase the modifiabiltiy, plasticity, and flexibility where inadequate because of the lack of MLE of general or specific nature. (The reader is referred to the vast literature on the subject. Several references appear in the Instrumental Enrichment addendum to the References [see Additional Resources].) It is important, however, to mention that this intervention program aims at developing the prerequisites of learning and correcting deficiencies in cognitive functions and operations. It provides a phase-specific substitute for insufficient or ineffective MLE. Its 300 hours of paper-pencil exercises are essentially non-content-specific and seek to transform the learner from a passive recipient of information to an active generator and projector of relationships. The material is taught three to five hours weekly over a two-to-three year period by teachers who have been specially trained as IE mediators. Positive results have been obtained in many of the 500 studies conducted across a broad range of populations and in a large variety of settings. The followup studies that have been carried out indicate that the modifiability that has occurred through this program is indeed structural in nature, as reflected in the permanence of the results and the divergent effects of the program manifesting itself in the continuation of its effects, after the cessation of the program.

Finally, the shaping of modifying environments is the third area derived from the theory of Structural Cognitive Modifiability and its pivotal element, MLE. This development of our program is rather recent and we are now striving to create a conceptual framework to outline the principles, rules, and nature of a modifying environment. It sets out to capitalize on the individual's unveiled modifiability, as evaluated by the LPAD and increased by the IE, in order to continue to modify the individual in the most adequate and desirable way.

It would be superfluous to say that not all environments can modify the individual; nor do all of them attempt or mean to do so. The successful unraveling of an individual's modifiability and its increase through the LPAD and IE may be without consequence or value if one does not ensure that the environment itself produces in the individual the need system that will make modifiability and its subsequent adaptability a survival social need. The search for means of ensuring the shaping of a modifying environment becomes extremely important.

As we have said elsewhere (Feuerstein and Hoffman 1982), MLE is the imposition of a culture that creates in the individual powers of adaptation in response to the needs present in the environment. Thus, it is MLE that is the interaction that ties together the three applied systems that are oriented toward the generation of human intelligence through the realization of the human propensity to change. Beyond this, we consider MLE to be a crucial determinant in human existence. The motive that is responsible for generating MLE as a modality of inter- and intra-generational interaction is clearly the need of human beings to see their existence continued beyond their limited biological life. This motive, often hidden, acts on the individual as well as the group level, where it appears as an explicit and clearly stated motive. Survival as an individual entity is paralleled by the survival of one's cultural identity. It is only through this motive that mediational interaction on the individual level and cultural transmission on the group level will find the means by which the mediation necessary for survival will be activated. This need generates concern for both the physical and spiritual nature of the human and guarantees the emotional, cognitive, and active involvement of the older generation in its progeny's future. This involvement projects itself from the depths of the past to the future of humanity. If, indeed, MLE has such an impact on both the life of individuals and on their emotional and moral engagement toward their progeny, then many changes may have to be produced in our way of organizing society, so as to create optimal conditions for mediational interactions. We may have to revise the idea of intergenerational discontinuity and counterculture in favor of a strong planned and controlled linkage between generations, particularly when life may tend to steer generations apart. In the modern world, there may have to be a different approach to instructional, educational, and social organization to create greater opportunities for intergenerational interaction and cultural transmission.

REFERENCES

Allman, W. F. 1989. The first humans. *U.S. News and World Report*, February 27, 52–59.

Beck, R. H. 1965. *A social history of education*. Englewood Cliffs, N.J.: Prentice-Hall, 97–99.

Bergson, H. 1956. *Matiere et memoire: Essai sur la relation du corps à l'esprit* (1919). Paris: Press Universitaires de France. 54th ed.

Detterman, D. K. and Sternberg, R. J. eds. 1982. *How and how much can intelligence be increased?* Norwood, N.J.: Ablex.

Eisenstadt, S. N. 1964. *The absorption of immigrants*. London: Routledge & Kegan Paul.

Emerson, L. 1985. *To sing our own songs: Cognition and culture in Indian education*. Report from a workshop for American Indian educators on the Learning Potential Assessment Device and Instrumental Enrichment programs. Shiprock, Navajo Nation, N.M. (Unpublished manuscript to be published by Freund, London.) New York: Association on American Indian Affairs in cooperation with the NiHa'Alchini Ba Educational Center, Shiprock, N.M.

Emerson, L. 1986, August. Feuerstein's MLE and American Indian education. Paper presented at Mediated Learning Experience International Workshop. Jerusalem, Israel.

Feuerstein, R. and Hoffman, M. B. 1982. Intergenerational conflict of rights: Cultural imposition and self-realization. *Viewpoints in Teaching and Learning, Journal of the School of Education* 58, no. 1.

Gardner, H. 1983. *Frames of mind: The theory of multiple intelligences*. New York: Basic Books.

Garrett, H. E.; Bryan, A. I.; and Perl, R. E. 1935. The age factor in mental organization. *Archives of Psychology*, no. 176.

Hebb, D. O. 1949. *The organization of behavior.* New York: John Wiley & Sons.

Hunt, J. McV. 1961. *Intelligence and experience.* New York: Ronald Press.

Jensen, A. R. 1987. Psychometric g as a focus of concerted research effort. *Intelligence* 11, July-September: 193–98.

Juliebo, M. F. 1985. The literacy world of five young children. *Language Arts* 62, no. 8: 848–56.

Kaniel, S.; Tzuriel, D.; Feuerstein, R.; Ben Shachar, N.; and Eitan, T. 1986. *Dynamic assessment: Learning and transfer abilities of Ethiopian immigrants to Israel.* Jerusalem: Hadassah-Wizo-Canada Research Institute and Ramat Gan: School of Education, Bar Ilan University.

Klein, P., and Feuerstein, R. 1985. Environmental variables and cognitive development. Identification of the potent factors in adult-child interaction. In *The at-risk infant,* ed. Sh. Harel and N. J. Anastasiow. Baltimore & London: Paul Brookes Publishing Co.

Kron, T. 1986. *Personal communication,* November 5.

Leemann, R. A. 1989. December 7. Aspekte das menschliche denken. *Neue Zuricher Zeitung,* p. 22.

Lesser, G. S.; Fifer, G.; and Clark, D. H. 1965. *Mental abilities of children of different social class and cultural groups.* Chicago: University of Chicago Press for the Society for Research in Child Development.

Minick, N. 1986. The development of Vygotsky's thought. Introduction to L. S. Vygotsky, *Collected Works. Problems of general psychology.* Vol. 1. New York: Plenum.

Minick, N. 1987. Implications of Vygotsky's theories for dynamic assessment. In *Dynamic assessment: An interactional approach to evaluating learning potential,* ed. C. S. Lidz, 116–38. New York and London: Guilford Press.

Piaget, J. 1970. In *Piaget's theory in Carmichael's Manual of child psychology,* ed. P. H. Mussen, 703–32. Vol. 1. New York: John Wiley.

Rosen, H. 1986. Series of articles on Ethiopian immigrants. Jerusalem: Hadassah Council in Israel.

Sameroff, A. J., and Chandler, M. J. 1975. Reproductive risk and the continuum of caretaking casualty. In *Review of child development research*, ed. F. D. Horowitz, 187–244. Chicago: University of Chicago Press.

Scheffler, I. 1985. *Of human potential: An essay in the philosophy of education.* Boston, London, Melbourne, and Henley: Routledge & Kegan Paul.

Sternberg, R. J. 1985. *Beyond IQ: A triarchic theory of human intelligence.* New York: Cambridge University Press.

Vygotsky, L. S. 1962. *Thought and language.* Ed. and trans. Eugenia Hanfmann and Gertrude Vakar. Cambridge, Mass.: Massachusetts Institute of Technology Press.

Wertsch, J. V. 1984. The zone of proximal development: Some conceptual issues. In *Children's learning in the "zone of proximal development,"* ed. B. Rogoff and J.V. Wertsch, 7–18. San Francisco: Jossey-Bass.

ADDITIONAL RESOURCES

Readers may find the additional resources on Professor Feuerstein's *Instrumental Enrichment* program of interest for applying his ideas in the classroom. First, a brief, up-to-date bibliography on the *Instrumental Enrichment* program is provided. Then, a list of the criteria and categories of interaction in Mediated Learning Experience (MLE) is provided, including the letter code used in the program and in research about the program.

INSTRUMENTAL ENRICHMENT (IE)
Bibliography

Feuerstein, R.; Rand, Y.; and Hoffman, M. B. 1979. *The dynamic assessment of retarded performers: The Learning Potential Assessment Device, theory, instruments, and techniques.* Glenview, Ill.: Scott, Foresman.

Feuerstein, R.; Rand, Y.; Hoffman, M. B.; and Miller, R. 1980. *Instrumental Enrichment: An intervention program for cognitive modifiability.* Baltimore, Md.: University Park Press.

Feuerstein, R.; Jensen, M.; Hoffman, M. B.; and Rand, Y. 1985. Instrumental Enrichment, an intervention program for structural cognitive modifiability: Theory and practice. In *Thinking and learning skills.* Vol. 1, *Relating instruction to research,* ed. J. W. Segal, S. F. Chipman, and R. Glaser. Hillsdale, N.J.: Lawrence Erlbaum.

Link, F. R. 1985. Instrumental Enrichment: Strategies for intellectual and academic improvement. In *Essays on the intellect,* ed. F. R. Link, 89–106. Alexandria, Va.: Association for Supervision and Curriculum Development.

Feuerstein, R.; Rand, Y.; and Rynders, J. E. 1988. *Don't accept me as I am: Helping "retarded" people to excel.* New York and London: Plenum Press.

MEDIATED LEARNING EXPERIENCE (MLE)
Criteria and Categories of Interaction and Code

The following is a brief blueprint of the encoding of MLE interactions according to their mediative meaning. It represents, for didactic purposes, a shortened version of suggested categories. As such, it is not to be considered as either exhaustive or definitive. (See *Instrumental Enrichment* 1980, Chapter 2).

I. CRITERIA FOR MLE

1. IR Intentionality and Reciprocity
2. T Transcendence
3. MM Mediation of Meaning
4. MFC Mediation of Feeling of Competence
5. MRCB Mediation Regulation and Control of Behavior
6. MSB Mediated Sharing Behavior
7. MIPD Mediated Individuation and Psychological Differentiation
8. MGSSA Mediation of goal seeking, goal setting and goal planning and achieving behavior
9. MCNC Mediation of challenge: the search for novelty and complexity
10. MAHCE Mediation of an awareness of the human as a changing entity
11. MOA Mediation of an optimistic alternative
12. MFB Mediation of the feeling of belonging

II. PARTICIPANTS AND INITIATORS IN MEDIATED INTERACTION

1. MC Mother Child (for ascendants add G)
2. CM Child Mother
3. FC Father Child
4. CF Child Father
5. CS Child Sibling
6. SC Sibling Child
7. CCT Child Caretaker
8. CTC Caretaker Child
9. CO Child Other
10. OC Other Child

III. CATEGORIZATION OF MEDIATED INTERACTIONS AND RESPECTIVE CODE

1. MF — Mediated Focusing
2. MSS — Mediated Selection of Stimuli
3. MS — Mediated Scheduling
4. PM — Provoking (requesting) Mediation
5. MPA — Mediation of Positive Anticipation
6. MAS — Mediated Act Substitute
7. MIM — Mediated Imitation
8. MRE — Mediated Repetition
9. MRR — Mediated Reinforcement and Reward
10. MVS — Mediated Verbal Stimulation
11. MIC — Mediated Inhibition and Control
12. MPS — Mediated provision of Stimuli
13. MRS — Mediated Recall Short-term
14. MRL — Mediated Recall Long-term
15. MTP — Mediated Transmission of Past
16. MRF — Mediated Representation of Future
17. MIDV — Mediated Identification and Description Verbal
18. MIDN — Mediated Identification and Description Non-verbal
19. PVRM — Positive Verbal Response to Mediation
20. PNVM — Positive Non-verbal Response to Mediation
21. MAR — Mediated Assuming Responsibility
22. MSR — Mediated Shared Responsibility
23. MCER — Mediation of Cause and Effect Relationship
24. MRV — Mediated Response Verbal
25. MRM — Mediated Response Motor

26. MDS Mediated Discrimination and Sequencing

27. MSO Mediation of Spatial Orientation

28. MTO Mediation of Temporal Orientation

29. MCB Mediation of Comparative Behavior

30. MSC Mediation Fostering a Sense of Completion

31. MDA Mediation Directing Attention

32. MAA Mediated Association and Application

33. MCI Mediated Critical Interpretation

34. MDR Mediated Deductive Reasoning

35. MIR Mediated Inductive Reasoning

36. MDIT Mediation Developing Inferential Thinking

37. MPSS Mediation of Problem-Solving Strategies

38. MTV Mediated Transmission of Values

39. MNPIL Mediation of Need of Precision on Input Levels

40. MNPOL Mediation of Need of Precision of Output Levels

41. MNLEI Mediation of Need of Logical Evidence on Input Levels

42. MNLEO Mediation of Need for Logical Evidence on Output Levels

43. MSE Mediation of Systematic Exploration

44. MCR Mediated Confrontation of Reality

45. MOS Mediated Organization of Stimuli

46. MCOV Mediation of Cognitive Operation Verbal

47. MCOM Mediation of Cognitive Operation Motor

48. MPFV Mediation of Perception of Feelings Verbal

49. MPFN Mediation of Perception of Feelings Non-verbal

50. MR Mediation of Reciprocity

IV. ADDITIONAL TYPES OF INTERACTIONS WITH STIMULI AND OTHERS

1. DEXIS   Direct Exposure and Interaction with Stimuli
2. PM   Interaction with Previously Mediated Stimuli
3. TE   Trial and Error
4. SOL   Soliloquy
5. NMI   Non-Mediated Interaction
6. NMAS   Non-Mediated Interaction leading to Substitute
7. NMVC   Non-Mediated Verbal Control
8. NMMC   Non-Mediated Motor Control

Chapter 5

SOME POSSIBLE ANSWERS: IMPLICATIONS FOR SCHOOLING AND PRACTICE

by Barbara Z. Presseisen

Answers to questions raised in the first chapter are sought first through an analysis of each theorist's position and then by examining practical aspects of current education and schooling. Changes in curriculum, instruction, and assessment are considered and compared to the theoretical positions. In a final note, social and philosophical implications of the emerging paradigm change in education are presented.

BUILDING BRIDGES

The great challenge of this book is to follow the three incisive studies presented by the educational theorists with meaningful discussion that relates their ideas to the questions raised in the first chapter. Coming from their specific interests and research, what can be learned from their positions that applies to real educational practice? What ideas have they stressed that relate to the concerns of educators in this era of reform or reconstruction?

Sternberg on Intellectual Styles

Robert Sternberg is well known for his insightful understanding of how people think, as well as how they develop their various mental abilities (Sternberg 1986). In the second

135

chapter of this volume, his position on the origins of intelligence and the breadth of human thought-making are extended to considerations of intellectual styles and individual tendencies toward style preference. Styles are key to actual performance, says Sternberg, not unrelated to ability but not dependent on it either. Styles are part of a learner's conative make-up, akin to what he/she is comfortable with, familiar with, and does naturally, and as such style becomes a bridge or connecting link between personality and intellectual functioning.

In terms of the questions initially raised in this volume (in the first chapter)—what is intelligence and how does a person develop competence?—Sternberg easily interjects his notions of intellectual style. Intelligence involves developed cognitive abilities; styles entail the dispositions and willingness actually to use these abilities. Sternberg sees both types of human characteristics as primarily socialized phenomena, and, since they are developed within a context of human exchange, they are both prone to modifiability and alteration.

Sternberg is known for his depiction of analogical reasoning, too, and the discussion of intellectual styles employs the metaphor of government for realizing the full dimensions or levels of human mental capacity: ". . . rather than attempting to understand governments in terms of the psychology of human beings, we are trying to understand the psychology of human beings in terms of governments" (p. 21). Sternberg thus links a person's ability to govern him/herself with multiple aspects that influence ways in which people organize or direct their intelligence. He names five such aspects; function, form, level, scope, and leaning, and he describes people he knows well, including himself, in terms of their variation on these simultaneous, interactive dimensions.

Compared to other academic depictions of style, which he reviews briefly but succinctly, Sternberg interrelates the five combinations of stylistic depiction in much more complex ways—as in playing the several layers of the Japanese game of Go.

A person can interweave his/her behavior across a broad spectrum of potential style choices, all at the same time, and relative to a number of contents. Although individuals tend to specialize in one aspect or another, Sternberg suggests that people prefer styles that capitalize on their strengths. They often exhibit predilection for a particular style because they are "at home" with similar kinds of behavior or types of action. In short, according to Sternberg, people use styles they have learned to perform well.

Sternberg creates an understanding of human behavior in complex ways based on style much as Gardner has discussed intelligence from multiple dimensions or Eisner has proposed ways of regarding several kinds of literacy (Gardner 1983; Eisner 1987). When style is seen through such an array of possibilities, the concept of *potential* becomes all the more possible. There are numerous ways that a student can act upon or exhibit his/her intelligence; how comfortable or inclined might he/she be to do so? How supportive is the learning environment to help him/her enact a particular style? In his view of the psychology of learning, Sternberg sees style generally independent of intelligence itself, except where it is constrained by the particular domain or content. It seems some kinds of knowledge require or relate to particular ways of dealing with that knowledge—calling for a heavier use of systematic rule behavior, for example, or an emphasis on analyzing specific relationships. But Sternberg also proposes that we actually learn best from people, and presumably from experiences, that are moderately unlike ourselves. There is a need for challenge and stretching in developing cognitive ability; heterogeneity helps to extend a learner's mental purview. At the same time, Sternberg proposes, too much dissonance in style or too unfamiliar a domain actually can preclude mental growth and thus turn off learning.

When dealing with the question of where the different stylistic concerns of intellectual functioning come from, Sternberg names at least six sources. He does not discount an inherited base, but he suggests that, at the same time, other factors are also at work on an individual learner. He lists culture, gender, age, parenting style, and kind of schooling as these key factors. One can see that any given person is a unique blend of influences, not only from his/her genetic inheritance, but also from a host of possible social experiences represented by an array of conditions related to the various factors. If a learner becomes aware of the power behind his/her own influential factors, he/she may become more likely to use and understand these influences over his/her developing styles. In line with Gardner's "personal intelligences" (1983, p. 237 ff.), the learner may comprehend the useful interrelationships between a preferred style and the actual deployment of intellectual abilities. In Sternberg's terms, such a learner can become more self-regulative of his/her own intelligence.

At one level, Sternberg's theory of intellectual styles is very similar to Edward de Bono's conception of *Six Thinking Hats* (de Bono 1985). De Bono postulates six different types of thinking that are available to every thinker. The types of thinking present different functions: dealing with emotion (red), raising constructive questions for new information (white), playing the devil's advocate (black), being positive and upbeat (yellow), developing creative solutions (green), and planning and organizing thoughtfully (blue). Using the different color hats interchangeably becomes a kind of flexible response system for de Bono, and similarly, for Sternberg, readily moving among style aspects can become a key to successful problem solving (p. 27). People need to use the different style aspects for different ends, to find out what works and why; the first step is a pragmatic "hands-on" doing, the second phase requires reflection and mental re-processing. That's how human beings learn from their mistakes, as well as their successes (Kamii 1984). Sometimes an alternate view, lateral thinking to de Bono, helps create a new feeling or attitude that enables a different solution to emerge, one that was not conceived of earlier. A change of style may be even more crucial to learning than a serious alteration of intellect.

Willingness to try something new, to deal with the novel, to be a risk-taker or a persistent inquirer, may be the source of intellectual breakthroughs that finally dislodge a difficult problem solution.

Sternberg holds up a fascinating mirror to the minds of thoughtful persons. His theory of intellectual styles conceives of thinkers as very practical people. His model presents an elegant design for fathoming the most intricate computer of them all, the human psyche. What is taught can be delivered in many configurations, just as how it is taught is open to all kinds of presentations. The one clear message that Sternberg's theory gives us is that there is no one truth for our understanding of how humans think and use their mental processes. Thinking and learning in a stylish way are at the heart of a dynamic conception of human ability.

Fischer and Knight on Skill Theory

Kurt Fischer and Catharine Knight have set out to draw a more complete map of how children cognitively change as they develop into mature thinkers. They suggest that other descriptions of this development have been overly simplistic and have failed to capture the right variation that every learner actually exhibits. Fischer and Knight call their theoretical framework "skill theory;" it is a neo-Piagetian approach. Central to their thesis is the constant variation of children's learning amidst alternative contexts and alternating states. There may be a sequence of uniform stages of development, they say, which all youngsters ultimately traverse, but *real children* are continually affected by context and experience, and "vary from moment to moment in terms of capacity, motivation, and emotional state" (p. 44). These two researchers have moved the Genevan ideas along a new pathway.

Skill theory is premised on a notion of dynamic interaction. It looks upon behavior as a constant interplay between a subject and his/her environment, and it assumes that such change is limited by a careful understanding of what the structure of attendant skills is to a child's growing cognition. There are upper demarcations that delimit how far a particular skill can be developed, and it is this optimal functioning that actually marks the stage achievement of any group of learners— "most behavior does not show stagelike change" (p. 45)—that is left for real children.

Fischer and Knight have developed a roadmap of optimal cognitive levels, arranged in a sequential hierarchy, and coordinated in a periodic time frame. The seven levels that they identify between 2 and 30 years of age are each characterized by an important step in cognitive developmental mastery. School begins when children are just starting to develop an understanding of systematic organization in their thought development. Early adolescence in middle schools is a period that requires the coordination of multiple concrete operations and grasping the significance of interrelated patterns, parts, and representational subsets. By the time they leave school after graduation, at 17 or 18 years of age, successful students have integrated a number of mental operations that make abstract systems possible to them. In a word, they have successfully reconstructed their own cognitive reality.

With regard to the question of *how* students manifest cognitive change, Fischer and Knight suggest it is in both continuous and discontinuous patterns. The change is relevant to ideal supportive conditions; thus there are many ordinary days when no alteration is obvious. But there are also growth or spurt periods when more generalized understandings are processed, when relationships are drawn, and about which learners become reflective. That is when optimal performance emerges. Adey in London reported similar findings among adolescent learners in an experimental science curriculum (Adey 1989). These researchers suggest that if we want to see students' very best performance, it is necessary to set the expectation and conditions for such an outcome. By the same token, educators must realize that what is seen most often in the classroom is merely functional, relatively spontaneous behavior.

Fischer and Knight draw a difference between students being able to produce a behavior on their own and performing it under high support conditions. They cite the work of the Vygotskian school on "the zone of proximal development," or ZPD in the current literature (Vygotsky 1962; Rogoff and Wertsch 1984). They focus on the internalization demands of specific task performance, studying how children interact with more experienced members in a group as they learn. Like Vygotsky, they suggest that how the work is organized within the group experience is an essential aspect of learning new tasks. Individual students have different experiences in the constellations of social interaction. Thus, for Fischer and Knight, individual differences with regard to outcomes is the norm in learners' development.

The area of developing reading skills is a useful example from Fischer and Knight for understanding their skill theory in the context of classroom interaction. They note that each child develops skill very differently compared to others in a class. Experiences differ, emotions and interests are dissimilar, and special facilities or disabilities on each child's part enter into his/her development of reading competence. Tasks need to be understood and instruction matched to student need—as in the integration of visual and sound information in early reading ability. Classroom support starts with a recognition task on the child's part of what the skill actually entails, before the learner can even begin to deal with how to perform or produce the particular skill. When that awareness has begun, then the learner is ready to move along to more complex tasks. Fischer and Knight note that the dyslexic performer is actually learning in a different developmental sequence compared to the so-called normal learners in a class.

Fischer and Knight postulate that their theory speaks to an awareness of the gradual building up of competence or ability on the learner's part. Like Sternberg's self-regulatory awareness, their discussion about Reflective Judgment assessment tools outlines the learner's slow, constructive self-education on the intricacies of the new knowledge as conceptual control is developed. All children will not be able to manifest such understanding—but those who do will reach the optimal level of learning in the given domain. The point that Fischer and Knight make with regard to the classroom support for such learning is that the sequence of task learning in any domain requires instructional support geared to each student's individual profile. For these two researchers, such concern and knowledge is central to a teacher's professional expertise.

Feuerstein's Theory of Structural Cognitive Modifiability

Reuven Feuerstein casts his net very widely in approaching the questions of development and learning in human cognitive functioning. There are many issues that need to be addressed, but two seem more central than all the others: What is intelligence? How does it come about? After a lifetime of research and implementation, he carefully addresses the first question:

> . . . intelligence should be defined as a process broad enough to embrace a large variety of phenomena that have in common the dynamics and mechanics of adaptation. (p. 71)

Feuerstein counters the static view of intelligence as a stable entity. Instead, he sees it as a dynamic, developing, interactive, changeable characteristic. And further, he suggests that what is most human and most creative about people of all ages, under many different kinds of circumstances, is that they are modifiable. Modifiability may differ from person to person, from state to state, from situation to situation, but the fact that it is so central to human development makes it a primary link to human learning. Adaptability and modifiability create the plasticity, the

142

flexibility, whereby cognitive change can occur. For Feuerstein, these are the basic conditions that provide the rationale for education in general.

In terms of the second central question—how does intelligence come about?—Feuerstein focuses on the human interactive processes, notably on communication among social beings. Like Piaget, his mentor, Feuerstein is quite aware of each human being's biological base. The organism's innate condition sets limits and possibilities for every person. But Feuerstein sees the human's ability to change and develop as something beyond the powers of the initial, physiologically dominated creature of nature. Like animals, the human being must survive the natural world and adapt him/herself to develop "creature comforts." Beyond such basic adaptation, humans also develop a second-level modality for adaptability and change, a system that ferrets out special types of situations that are meaningful and instructive, and which enables the reflective learner to organize his/her behaviors and responses in much more productive ways. For the Israeli psychologist, the key to such a system is called mediated learning experience (MLE); it is the relationship *par excellence* between the teacher and the taught.

> Learners can benefit not only from the direct exposure to a particular stimulus, but they can also forge in themselves a repertoire of dispositions, propensities, orientations, attitudes, and techniques that enable them to modify themselves in relation to other stimuli . . . MLE is the determinant responsible for the development of the flexibility of the schemata which ensures that the stimuli that impinge on us will affect us in a meaningful way. (p. 75)

Meaningfulness to Feuerstein is a highly individualistic situation. In a similar fashion, learning ability—the propensity for learning—is also very individualized. Every learner can benefit from exposure to learning situations, the significant question is, what makes any particular learner interested or involved in such a situation? What leads to real interaction in a given environment? Feuerstein is obviously interested in Sternberg's styles and their influence on triggering intelligence. He is also cognizant of Fischer and Knight's supportive classroom settings—all of these concerns are part of a *mediated* learning relationship. MLE is the purposeful, intentional instructional system that turns randomly available stimuli into an appropriate encounter for a learner, so as to help him/her recognize, register, integrate, and master the particular contents of learning. The MLE experience is not the mere transfer of specific bits of information; it is a special happening that creates in the learner "a disposition, an attitudinal propensity to benefit from the direct exposure to stimuli" (p. 79). For Feuerstein, what a teacher is about is helping to build a capacity for learning in the child, to move the child in his/her individualistic way to a higher level of being able to adapt and change his/her thinking, to construct a new intellectual state. That is the structural dimension of Feuerstein's cognitive modifiability.

What Feuerstein ultimately comes to address is why whole groups of learners fail to reach higher-order thinking ability, the more sophisticated levels of intelligence. In other words, his theory is concerned not only with individual differences, with a complexity of situations that influence personal human learning, but with the causes of learning disability among groups of learners who are not tuned into academic studies and who sooner or later turn themselves out of formal schooling. He raises questions about how successfully mediated experiences are related to the culture and/or the segment of society in which any particular individual resides. Whereas, in the past, the family has been the main teaching agent of culture, Feuerstein finds that modern society has given that task to professional agents and, considering the role of mass media in modern life, to technological surrogates, as well. Have these occurrences made difficulty for socialization and enculturation processes? Indeed, he says, they have.

Feuerstein uses much of the research he has amassed in

Israel to tell of the possibilities of MLE as an important instructional approach for children in unusual learning circumstances. He distinguishes between two types of determinants of differential cognitive development: distal and proximal (see Figure 1 on p. 88). Distal determinants are factors like heredity, organicity, socioeconomic status—factors that are fairly distant from the learner *per se*, but active agents in the larger social context. Proximal factors are those that are closer or more attached to the learner, of immediate meaningfulness or personal impact. MLE is such a proximal factor. According to Feuerstein, MLE is an experience that enables an individual to respond flexibly to even the most radical or stressful of human occurrences and yet to maintain an individual sense of beingness, a self-identity. He sees MLE as transformation of one's ties with the past as well as the construction of a positive, personal future. With such a proximal experience, learning can take place. Without it, the ability to learn does not manifest itself, learning disability predominates. Feuerstein cites examples of MLE in a cultural setting in his review of Yemenite children moving to Israel. He shows how differently a child's question is answered when a teacher mediates compared to when simple, rhetorical responses are given. Mediation transcends the immediacy of the required interaction. A child points to an orange as a questioning act. The mediator says that it is the fruit of a tree, naming it and related items, and giving examples and illustrative conditions. The teacher presents to the learner answers with many more possibilities for relating the object in question to the child's entire perspective.

Feuerstein ascribes to MLE other aspects that influence both the cultural cognitive styles and emotional behaviors of learners. Among these, he includes mediation of a feeling of competence, mediation of regulation and control of behavior, mediation of sharing behavior, mediation of individuation and psychological differentiation, mediation of goal seeking, setting, planning, and achieving behavior, mediation for challenge, awareness of change, and mediation of an optimistic approach. In short, he agrees with Sternberg that "styles" related to human development concerns are, at least in part, socialized, and that such behaviors can be influenced separately from the nature of a given person's intellectual abilities or intelligence. Whatever a learner's distal condition, the possibilities for changing his/her proximal experience are great, and in doing so, there is a definite potential for influencing his/her cognitive development. Like Sternberg, Feuerstein proposes that the appropriate kind of mediated experience can, in fact, enhance a learner's modifiability, thus in a way teach intelligence itself.

Feuerstein highlights the need for MLE in drawing the distinction between culturally different and culturally deprived groups of learners. Children who are or have been seriously culturally deprived are devoid of prerequisites of learning, he says (see Figure 2 on pp. 108–9); hence they have a limited capacity to benefit from opportunities to advance or to change. These children are most marked by their episodic grasp of reality, although Feuerstein also has developed a long list of other related deficiencies. What has become most notable in the modern technological world, he suggests, is the inability of culturally deprived groups to become functional, productive workers in societies driven by higher skills and "smart machines." Feuerstein cites the problems of immigrant groups all over the world. He finds parallel populations of deficient thinkers in some Navajo Indian children of the United States and Jewish immigrants from Ethiopia, recently moved to Israel. In both cases, based on studies conducted by his research center in Jerusalem, MLE was provided by the implementation of Feuerstein's (1980) *Instrumental Enrichment* program, which made it possible to transform children bereft of learning into students who were motivated, successful, and competent thinkers. The Israeli psychologist maintains that the beginnings of literacy for such groups were rooted in the kinds of selective experiences that are taught by his program, and in the particular instructional ways fostered by the mediator-teachers. In these groups, even under the most difficult circumstances, it was possible to find children with a potential for learning, as tested by Feuerstein's (1979) *Learning Potential Assessment Device* (LPAD), and to create meaningful classroom experiences for them. It would seem that the supportive environments for learning and the sequence of Piaget-like tasks discussed by Fischer and Knight are highly parallel elements to the theory of cognitive modifiability proposed by Reuven Feuerstein.

IMPLICATIONS FOR SCHOOLING AND PRACTICE

In returning to the questions raised in the first chapter of this volume, it comes as no surprise that cognitive-developmental understanding of human learning sides with a dynamic view of human intelligence. Learning is a very complex, long-range mental task and the human thinker an awesome, critical, creative, and adaptable being. Children coming to school need to learn to do many things; they particularly need to become sophisticated in ways of knowing, often in terms far more intricate than they or even their teachers are able to describe fully.

The theorists whose studies are presented in the middle chapters of this book each describe in his/her way how humans change as they learn or adapt to the stimuli in their environment, as they learn to become competent thinkers. Sternberg focuses on intellectual styles as his approach to understanding complex mental processing, emphasizing that the unique background each child carries with him/her is a source of personal motivation that ultimately drives cognitive behavior. Fischer and Knight highlight skill development itself, emphasizing the transformation from mundane to more optimal performance, which occurs if and when supportive environments and carefully constructed social experiences are developed to nurture the nascent thinkers. Feuerstein stresses the mediational role of the teacher as the key ingredient of a positive exchange between expert and novice, couched in a cultural and sociological context, and focused on learning prerequisites that empower the student as a knower of his/her own reality. All these theorists adhere to the notion that, in the final analysis, the student must become the owner of his/her own ideas and the independent master of his/her own achievement. School is the supportive environment, particularly related to academic tasks—but not exclusively—in which such a transformation is supposed to take place.

In this era of educational reform, implications to be drawn from these new understandings about learning, thinking, and teaching naive students are not unrelated to real happenings in school practice. In fact, the paradigm shift mentioned in the initial chapter of this book may be related to the theoretical positions discussed, but just as importantly may touch on everyday happenings in schools and classrooms. What might these real situations be?

Curriculum and an Era of Change

The issues raised by the theorists in question really address the core concerns of a cognitive curriculum as currently discussed by a number of educational researchers (Presseisen 1987; Resnick and Klopfer 1989; Blythe and Gardner 1990). The paradigm shift facing school reformers today involves a programmatic challenge to move the school's agenda away from an emphasis on content coverage and mere knowledge accumulation to a perspective that is focused on complex forms of thinking and the centrality of meaning. It is a program that insists on both knowledge and engaged instruction, and it emphasizes the use of multiple intelligences and high content for all students. Even those who have traditionally been locked out of more sophisticated studies are included in this new perspective (Presseisen 1988a).

At the heart of the new view of curriculum *cum* thinking is an acceptance of constructivist-developmental psychology and

148

an appreciation that, over time, every student can become a more adept builder of his/her own knowledge system. "Hands-on learning" takes a more central role in the new curriculum, to be considered at the same time that the question "what knowledge is of most worth?" is addressed. One is reminded of Shulman's (1987) interest in both content knowledge and pedagogical decision making as dual concerns of the expert teacher. The need for curricular materials to be motivating to students, as well as keyed to appropriate developmental tasks, is an unspoken requisite of current curricular demands. In an age where education competes with television, compact discs, and electronic video games, the school's curriculum needs to be able to engage its clients and to carry their interests and applications beyond the walls of a particular classroom or school. The program of the school needs to address higher-order thinking in every content area and build curricula to help learners work in growing conceptual complexity, as cognitive processes are mastered within each knowledge domain (Presseisen 1988b).

The new view of curriculum conceives of the teacher's role very differently from the earlier program of information transfer. Feuerstein's emphasis on the teacher as mediator is quite different from the position of the instructor who possesses all the necessary knowledge and who is prepared merely to deliver it readily packaged to given students, sometimes in an arrogant manner. Sternberg's discussion of potential conflict between style preferences of teachers and students lays the base for the kinds of activities that are ultimately included in the successful classroom program. Today's curriculum looks first to the needs of the particular learners and then to generic thinking operations that all students need to encounter and master. Both Fischer and Knight's developmental tasks and Feuerstein's instruments of higher-order thinking development are candidates for the school's new curricular plan. Simple, finite answers are now less important in the school's program than questioning and determining how one arrives at particular conclusions—and more significantly—why.

Instruction and an Era of Change

With a new cognitive curriculum comes a changing view of classroom instruction. Activity and engagement on the learner's part are paramount in the new goals of instructional development, but such action needs to be focused on tasks that help the learner fathom the content and, at the same time, meaningfully interrelate the cognitive understanding of the particular domain. Hands-on learning experiences are seen as initial engagements to begin the mediational process. Social interaction during the learning process between and among teachers and students, including cooperative learning lessons, reciprocal teaching techniques, peer tutoring, and peer collaboration, are all means to enable learners to become active learners in egalitarian and mutually supportive environments (Johnson and Johnson 1989–1990; Slavin, Madden and Stevens 1989–1990). The goal of many of these new classroom instructional models is involved learners bent on *performing* learning *in situ* and continuously progressing in terms of a personal understanding of the specific content or lesson. Multiple styles of learning à la Sternberg, and supportive academic environments for learning at the optimal level, as envisioned by Fischer and Knight, are part of the new view of instruction.

The importance of social interaction as a given in classroom instruction highlights the significance of a Vygotskian influence on the new pedagogy. In the quest for proximal experience, teaching is defined as assistance performance, essentially the same view as Feuerstein's mediation in MLE. Teaching occurs when performance is achieved by the students with the teacher's assistance at first, and then independently as the learner becomes master of his/her own involvement (Tharp and Gallimore 1988; Rogoff and Wertsch 1984). The new socially based instructional activities need to be designed to allow

150

teachers to assist children through the zone of proximal development, toward the goal of developing higher-order thinking about the contents involved. These kinds of settings are to engage students in goal-oriented actions in which the teacher and the student's classmates become co-participants in learning. The teacher assists and monitors each child as an individual learner. Ideally, students move from other regulation to self-regulation and, eventually, to internalization and full understanding (Brophy 1986). Bruner (1985) sees an instrumentalism in the Vygotskian base; thought and language are instruments the learner uses for building cognitive skill, metacognitive awareness, and conative commitment, while planning and carrying out action in the learning process. In the same way, Feuerstein (1980) sees his intervention program, *Instrumental Enrichment*, as a cognitive base for students who have difficulty in learning and whose life experience is unable to enlighten them on the fine nuances of academic understanding.

The new instructional focus emphasizes the importance of integrating motivation to learn with the ability to manage one's own learning. Numerous researchers stress the need to ally skill and will in the concept of self-regulation (McCombs and Marzano 1989; Zimmerman and Schunk 1989). Self-regulatory activity becomes a central focus of specific content instruction, applications are often advocated in teaching regular school subjects (Palincsar and Brown 1989). With such a goal in mind, the need for students to see a variety of coping strategies in operation justifies grouping children with different abilities in common work settings. Sternberg's notion that children learn best in heterogeneous learning situations, and Fischer and Knight's emphasis on the discontinuous occurrence of optimal performance, highlight the need to give all students the richest and gradually diverse instructional experience possible. Students also need time to internalize the new models of thinking, to practice them on their own and in the privacy of their own minds. The new instructional paradigm is one of high skill, high content, and high enthusiasm. It is a matter of high challenge to today's educators, too, particularly in the most needy instructional environments.

Assessment and an Era of Change

Like the need of curriculum and instruction for reorganization to adjust to a very different educational climate in America, it is not surprising that assessment, too, has some very different needs under education's new paradigm. Concerned with addressing that which is essential in the content of the curriculum, the new cognitive assessment is also bent on dealing with authentic processes of learning and understanding what is studied at school (Baron 1989; Wiggins 1989). The focus of educational achievement in the newer approaches to learning is a concern for proficient *performance* and the encouragement of students to improve their own abilities and skillfulness to master the best approximation of such performance (Cole 1990).

In contrast to previous assessment practices, the new paradigm emphasizes changes in students' understanding, closely allied with cognitive development of the intricacies of a particular subject matter. Long-term change is underlined in this approach, as the gradual development of expertise and the ability to communicate and elaborate new understandings grow. Keeping logs of students' work, developing portfolios of project activities and products, and building a variety of teacher and district records of student progress mark success in the new assessment. In contrast to this model are the normed test scores, the decontextualized learnings sampled in short answer–multiple choice items, and the single answer responses unsubstantiated and separated from actual classroom experience in the more traditional, and perhaps ineffective, practices of the recent past.

Sternberg's intellectual styles can easily be related to the newer approaches to assessment, as they become a means to focus student work and provide an alternative route to sample performance in a given student's preferred mode of thinking. Project development that is naturally allied with desired optimal performance could synchronize assessment and curricular goals in one educational effort, much as Fischer and Knight call for the need to support optimal classroom arrangements. Students ultimately need to be able to judge their own efforts, to monitor their own progress, and to be able to communicate what the new assessment calls public criteria of success (Gitomer 1989). Teachers and students obviously have to build a common understanding about such performance goals.

The new assessment practices call for a renewed involvement of teachers in actual testing practices, and in the deliberation about what constitutes successful mastery of subject matter, as well. Feuerstein (1979) underlines the need to assess what a given child's potential is in a particular learning situation, and he has developed a whole new dynamic approach to assessment to aid the teacher in defining the needs of further instruction. Such practices in dynamic assessment are already a part of the larger literature on cognitive instruction and curriculum (Campione and Brown 1987; Lidz 1987; Kletzien and Bendar 1990). Slowly but surely, the new paradigm seems to be falling in place.

A Final Note

The current educational reform era turns ultimately on what happens between teachers and students, as well as among learners, in the classroom and throughout a school building. In an age that calls for workers to think smarter (Zuboff 1988), and for disadvantaged students to share equitably in the cultural heritage for the good of society at large, classroom interaction is the focus of learning and—according to the theorists reviewed in this study—the development of intelligence itself. The student is an important participant and monitor of that active process.

The role of the teacher as mediator, model, and mentor

is central to the new paradigm of education. But the instructor of students who will work most of their adult lives in the twenty-first century is no longer an authoritarian "sage on the stage." As builder of a supportive social environment, as manager of a climate for inquiry, the teacher's primary task is to engage the minds of students in meaningful ways, such that they become the constructors of their own learning. Their styles of knowing and thinking, and the teacher's as well, are important aspects of their personal involvement and growth in the experience of education.

What the new paradigm of education seems to be calling into place are the requisites of a more democratic society built into the institution of schooling itself. To paraphrase John Dewey, what is emerging today is a type of education that will give individual students a personal interest in their own learning—and control over it—along with the mental abilities to secure social and intellectual changes and development without introducing disorder. Are America's classrooms so far away from those of Prague, Budapest, and Vilnius?

A period of reform is an exciting and challenging time to live in.

REFERENCES

Adey, P. 1989. *Cognitive acceleration through science education.* Conference report. Paris: Organization for Economic Cooperation and Development (OECD), (photocopy).

Baron, J. B. 1989, March. Toward a new generation of student outcome measures: Connecticut's common core of learning assessment. Paper presented at the annual meeting of the American Educational Research Association, San Francisco (photocopy).

Blythe, T., and Gardner, H. 1990, April. A school for all intelligences. *Educational Leadership* 47 no. 1: 33–36.

de Bono, E. 1985. *Six thinking hats.* London: Penguin Books.

Brophy, J. 1986, October. Teacher influences on student achievement. *American Psychologist* 41, no. 10: 1069–77.

Bruner, J. 1985. Vygotsky: A historical and conceptual perspective. In *Culture, communication, and cognition,* ed. J. V. Wertsch. New York: Cambridge University Press.

Campione, J. C., and Brown, A. L. 1987. Linking dynamic assessment with school achievement. In *Dynamic assessment: An interactional approach to evaluating learning potential,* ed. C. S. Lidz. New York: Guilford Press.

Cole, N. S. 1990, April. Conceptions of educational achievement. *Educational Researcher* 19, no. 3: 2–7.

Eisner, E. W. 1987, Fall. The celebration of thinking. *Educational Horizons* 66, no. 1: 24–29.

Feuerstein, R. 1979. *The dynamic assessment of retarded performers: The learning potential assessment device, theory, instruments and techniques.* Glenview, Ill.: Scott, Foresman.

Feuerstein, R. 1980. *Instrumental enrichment: An intervention program for cognitive modifiability.* In collaboration with Y. Rand, M. B. Hoffman, and R. Miller. Baltimore: University Park Press.

Gardner, H. 1983. *Frames of mind: The theory of multiple intelligences.* New York: Basic Books.

Gitomer, D. 1989, November. Developing a portfolio culture that enables learners. Paper presented at the National Summit Conference on the Arts and Education. New York: John F. Kennedy Center for the Performing Arts (photocopy).

Johnson, D. W., and Johnson, R. T. 1989, December-1990, January. Social skills for successful group work. *Educational Leadership* 47, no 4: 29–33.

Kamii, C. 1984. Autonomy: The aim of education envisioned by Piaget. *Phi Delta Kappan* 65, no. 6: 410–15.

Kletzien, S. B., and Bendar, M. R. 1990, April. Dynamic assessment for at-risk readers. *Journal of Reading* 33, no. 7: 528–33.

Lidz, C. S. 1987. *Dynamic assessment: An interactional approach to evaluating learning potential.* New York: Guilford Press.

McCombs, B. L. and Marzano. R. 1989, September-October. Integrating skills and will in self-regulation. *Teaching thinking and problem solving* 11, no. 5: 1–4.

Palincsar, A. S., and Brown, A. L. 1989. Instruction for self-regulated reading. In *Toward a thinking curriculum: Current cognitive research*, ed. L. B. Resnick and L. E. Klopfer. Alexandria, Va.: Association for Supervision and Curriculum Development.

Presseisen, B. Z. 1987. *Thinking skills throughout the curriculum: A conceptual design.* Bloomington, Ind.: Pi Lambda Theta.

Presseisen, B. Z., ed. 1988a. *At-risk students and thinking.* Washington, D.C. and Philadelphia: National Education Association and Research for Better Schools.

Presseisen, B. Z. 1988b, April. Avoiding battle at Curriculum Gulch: Teaching thinking and content. *Educational Leadership* 45, no. 7: 7–8.

Resnick, L. B., and Klopfer, L. E. 1989. Toward the thinking curriculum: An overview. In *Toward a thinking curriculum: Current cognitive research*, ed. L. B. Resnick and L. E. Klopfer, 1–18. Alexandria, Va.: Association for Supervision and Curriculum Development.

Rogoff, B. and Wertsch, J. V., eds. 1984. *Children's learning in the "Zone of Proximal Development."* San Francisco: Jossey-Bass.

Shulman, L. S. 1987. Knowledge and teaching: Foundations of the new reform. *Harvard Educational Review* 57, no. 1: 1–22.

Slavin, R. E.; Madden, N. A.; and Stevens, R. J. 1989, December–

1990, January. Cooperative learning modes for the 3 R's. *Educational Leadership* 47, no. 4: 22–28.

Sternberg, R. J. 1986. *Intelligence applied: Understanding and increasing your intellectual skills.* San Diego: Harcourt, Brace, Jovanovich.

Tharp, R. G., and Gallimore R. 1988. *Rousing minds to life: Teaching, learning, and schooling in social context.* New York: University Press.

Vygotsky, L. S. 1962. *Thought and language.* Translated by E. Hanfmann and G. Vakar. Cambridge, Mass.: MIT Press.

Wiggins, G. 1989, April. Teaching to the (authentic) test. *Educational Leadership* 46, no. 7: 41–47.

Zimmerman, B. J., and Schunk, D. H. 1989. *Self-regulated learning and academic achievement: Theory, research, and practice.* New York: Springer-Verlag.

Zuboff, S. 1988. *In the age of the smart machine.* New York: Basic Books.

THE CONTRIBUTORS

Barbara Z. Presseisen is Director of National Networking at Research for Better Schools in Philadelphia, the mid-Atlantic regional educational laboratory. She also serves as Chair of the Cross-Laboratory Committee on Higher Order Thinking Skills, and as contributing editor of the newsletter, *Teaching Thinking and Problem Solving*. Dr. Presseisen is the author of several books and numerous studies on cognitive development and curriculum. These include *Thinking Skills: Research and Practice* and *At-Risk Students and Thinking: Perspectives from Research* (of which she was editor), published by NEA. She has a special interest in the education of at-risk students and staff development concerns.

Robert J. Sternberg is the IBM Professor of Psychology and Education at Yale University. Well-known for his pioneering work in the study of human intelligence, Dr. Sternberg is a formidable figure in the movement to teach thinking at all levels of schooling. He is the author of numerous major studies in various topics of psychology from appraisals of IQ assessment to rich analyses of metacognition, intuition, critical thinking, and analogical understanding. Dr. Sternberg is a widely known lecturer and the developer of both assessment and instructional materials in the field of cognitive development.

Kurt W. Fischer is Professor of Education and Chair of Human Development and Psychology in the Graduate School of Education at Harvard University. He also serves as Director of the new Laboratory of Cognitive Development at the university. Dr. Fischer is a leading figure in research on children's cognitive development, with a particular focus on skill acquisition in content domains. His approach is known as Skill Theory. Dr. Fischer's recent studies focus on cognition, emotion, and behavior integrated in one general framework for predicting and

159

explaining changes in the organization of behavior. His interest in the relations between brain and cognition parallels exciting new efforts around the world in the field of cognitive neuroscience. Currently, Dr. Fischer also serves as president of the Jean Piaget Society.

Catharine C. Knight is an Assistant Professor of Developmental Psychology at Baldwin-Wallace College in Berea, Ohio. She served as a post-doctoral researcher with Kurt Fischer at the University of Denver. A specialist in the developmental approach to learning to read, Dr. Knight completed many of the field studies that formed the basis of data collection in their joint research.

Reuven Feuerstein is Professor of Developmental Psychology in the School of Education at Bar Ilan University in Ramat Gan, Israel, and Director of the Hadassah-WIZO-Canada Research Institute and the International Center for Structural Cognitive Modifiability in Jerusalem. He is internationally known for his seminal research on human development and performance, and for his ground-breaking work on new programs and interventions in the development of potential in children considered difficult to educate. Dr. Feuerstein is the primary author of *Instrumental Enrichment*, a thinking program in practice around the world, and the *Learning Potential Assessment Device* (LPAD), one of the innovative assessment programs in the developing area of dynamic assessment.